PENGUIN BU

# GETTING DRESSED AND PARKING CARS

Alok Kejriwal is a Mumbai-based serial digital entrepreneur and is currently the CEO and co-founder of Games2win. His first two companies, contests2win.com and Mobile2win, pioneered digital gaming and promotions in the world. The Walt Disney Company later acquired Mobile2win.

Besides being a businessperson, Alok is an Art of Living teacher and regularly facilitates meditation and breathing workshops. He has been practising meditation for the last thirty years.

Alok's first book, *Why I Stopped Wearing My Socks*, was a bestseller and won the C.K. Prahalad Best Business Book prize at the 2019 Bangalore Business Literature Festival. He is also a motivational speaker and has spoken at various corporate conferences, as well as at the Wharton School, the Harvard Business School, IIMs and IITs.

Alok takes a keen interest in mentoring emerging entrepreneurs and writes a popular daily blog #dhandhekibaat on Facebook and LinkedIn.

Website: http://games2winmedia.com
X (formerly Twitter): https://twitter.com/rodinhood
LinkedIn: https://www.linkedin.com/in/alokkejriwal/
Instagram: https://www.instagram.com/rodinhood/
Email: alok@rodinhood.com

Celebrating 35 Years of
Penguin Random House India

# GETTING DRESSED
### AND
# PARKING CARS

## The Magical Story of Building a Gaming Company

# ALOK KEJRIWAL

PENGUIN
BUSINESS

An imprint of Penguin Random House

PENGUIN BUSINESS

USA | Canada | UK | Ireland | Australia
New Zealand | India | South Africa | China | Singapore

Penguin Business is part of the Penguin Random House group of companies
whose addresses can be found at global.penguinrandomhouse.com

Published by Penguin Random House India Pvt. Ltd
4th Floor, Capital Tower 1, MG Road,
Gurugram 122 002, Haryana, India

First published in Penguin Business by Penguin Random House India 2023

Copyright © Alok Kejriwal 2023

All rights reserved

10 9 8 7 6 5 4 3 2 1

The views and opinions expressed in this book are the author's own and the
facts are as reported by him which have been verified to the extent possible,
and the publishers are not in any way liable for the same.

ISBN 9780143459170

Typeset in Arno Pro by Manipal Technologies Limited, Manipal

www.penguin.co.in

# Contents

*Offered at the Lotus Feet of Gurudev Sri Sri Ravishankar,
Mahavatar Babaji, Lord Bankey Bihari*

*In loving memory of Nana and Nani*

*Dedicated to Chhavi, Anushka and Amaya*

# Introduction

After successfully exiting my two mobile start-ups, Mobile2win China to Disney and Mobile2win India to Norwest Venture Partners for cash, I could have built anything I wanted to for my next venture.

I had the capital, the know-how, the reputation and, most importantly, the people. There were so many opportunities to choose from. You could say that I was spoilt for choice.

Yet, I chose to walk in the opposite direction. I spent time introspecting about becoming 'starved for choice'.

I made a long list of all the things I never wanted to do in my life and the failures that haunted me. I pondered over what I had not accomplished and the possible reasons behind it.

From this life-changing meditation, a great clarity emerged. By eliminating the many negatives, I was left with a few positives.

That's when I knew exactly what I wanted to do. I wanted to build a global, casual gaming company to entertain consumers worldwide.

This book is about that company and my fourth venture—Games2win. Each chapter in the book is true and recounts the experiences of building and scaling this start-up into a business. The narrative that follows is arranged into milestones along the exhilarating roller-coaster journey, with many surprises thrown in, in between.

Some of the stories include getting arrested, dealing with all our top games getting stolen, being sneaky and eating humble pie in San Francisco, looking for a CTO and finding a spouse, and living with the regret of missing out on tons of opportunities. Better secure your seat belt before you start reading!

The title refers to the two genres of games we pioneered and scaled at Games2win—dress-up games and car parking and driving games. These became our crown jewels that made our games win—Games2win!

The lessons at the end of each chapter are meant for all readers. This is not a book about start-ups or entrepreneurship so much as it is about the spirit of creating something new and getting started.

As I have seen repeatedly, taking the first step is the biggest achievement. Everything else follows.

I hope you enjoy reading this book and are inspired to do something unique of your own, just as I did with 'getting dressed and parking cars'.

Mumbai
1 September 2023

# 1

## *Neti, neti*

When I was thirteen, an uncle treated me to a Sunday poolside brunch in one of South Mumbai's five-star hotels. I loved the experience and kept dipping in and out of the pool while feasting on junk food.

That evening, my uncle asked me, 'Alok, what would you like to do when you are older?'

Giddy from my Sunday high, I impulsively said, 'Sit at a poolside and eat French fries.'

My uncle teased me for the next few months, often telling relatives and friends, 'Alok's plan for the future is to sit at a poolside and eat French fries!'

I hated him for this.

As I grew older, my teachers, guardians and a job interviewer asked me, 'What would you like to be ten or fifteen years from now?'

I was still trying to understand the question, clueless about how to attempt to answer it. How could any young person know this?

As I matured, I realized the question's inherent stupidity.

The intelligent question would have been, 'Alok, tell us everything you *don't* want to be ten or fifteen years from now. That way, we can help you figure out your plans!'

In Sanskrit, *'neti, neti'* means 'not this, not that'. It is a proven and prescribed method of negating options to arrive at the truth.

Neti, neti has been the framework for shaping my career and entrepreneurial journey. It has served me well.

I keep adding to a 'will not do' list as often as possible. And whenever I need to do something new, I find a magical answer by looking at this list.

Let me share how it works:

I had profitably exited two of my previous companies. Mobile2win China was acquired by Walt Disney Company and Mobile2win India was acquired by Norwest Venture Partners, a venture capital firm. (The nitty gritty is captured in my first book, *Why I Stopped Wearing My Socks*[*]).

Post both exits, I had plenty of capital, energy, two significant achievements as an entrepreneur and the burning desire to do much more.

I revised my neti, neti list to plot my third venture.

My first venture (in early 2000) was an Indian online contesting website called contests2win.com, which succeeded beyond my wildest dreams. This pioneering

---

[*]  Alok Kejriwal, *Why I Stopped Wearing My Socks*, Westland, 2018.

dot-com venture was an outstanding achievement but could not scale. Working with Fortune 500 clients was terrific, but it also had many negatives. These customers would demand my attention constantly, and the work became slavish. Instead of a contesting portal, I felt I was running an online advertising agency. I would not have lasted long doing this and realized this in time.

## Neti 1: Services as a business was never going to be my business.

My second venture (2000–2007) was Mobile2win. I migrated my online contesting business model to the first generation of mobile phones (Nokia phones), and the company took off. We set up shop in China with investment from the mighty SoftBank. This business was the one that the Walt Disney Company eventually acquired.

While we had remarkable success in China, the Indian division of Mobile2win also did exceedingly well. We pioneered 'SMS contesting' and powered India's 'Indian Idol' franchise, inspiring India to vote via SMS for the very first time.

Unfortunately, even though the company began to prosper, my success was cursed.

At Mobile2win, I was a business mentor and evangelist while my co-founders ran the company. As the money and success came rolling in, they plotted with shark-type venture capitalists (VCs) and ejected me from my own company. I was forced to accept a lucrative greenmail offer to get out and disappear.

**Neti 2: I would never start a business and remain a passive investor. I would run my own business with my hands and brains until the end.**

As I absorbed the shock of being thrown out of my own company, I pondered long and hard. I reflected that my entire entrepreneurial life of twenty-two years (I started working when I was sixteen) had been focused on building businesses *from India for India*.

While that model had delivered large business volume, plenty of publicity, PR and personal recognition, it had been a superficial success. I hadn't made a dent in the global markets. My profitability had always been razor-thin. The Indian markets were price-sensitive, with a deep-rooted '*paisa-vasool*' mindset. And whatever little early success came through, many smaller and cheaper copycats came after me and ruined the business model.

So I decided:

**Neti 3: I would no longer build from India for India. Instead, I would make from India for the world.**

My new adventure and the story of this book began with crystal clear pointers of what I did NOT want to do. With that clarity and mindset, I took my giant leap forward!

# LEARNINGS

- Practice neti, neti.
- Make a detailed list of what doesn't work for you—be it a business model, type of people to work with, a particular market or geography, culture or arrangement.
- By 'blacklisting' what you don't like, you can go about 'whitelisting' options and plot your way forward.

# 2

# Why, first

I began working when I was sixteen (in the family business) and developed a passion for working on new ideas, hoping to turn them into a business. It was an incredible journey trying to sell drums and discount letters of credit, transport goods and solve the problems of non-resident Indians (NRIs) applying for Indian IPOs. But none of these businesses went very far. There was an apparent reason for their failures, which I would only realize a few years later: all these business ventures failed because I had started them using the impulsive emotional triggers of 'who', 'what', 'where' and 'when'.

In all these, I had missed leveraging the critical, success-defining parameter of 'why'.

The post-mortem of my critical failures revealed:

-   I started a digital media services company called Media2win to help brands plan and execute digital marketing campaigns. My trigger was, 'I know all the top brands in the country, and they love what I do for them, so why not also offer them digital marketing.'

I was trying to make the 'who' the reason to succeed.

The agency failed. The 'who' (my clients) still loved me but did not care for my marketing services. My team did not meet the standards of the fierce competition in the market, and the business failed.

Instead, I should have asked, 'Why would clients who worked with me on creative ideas also work with me on their marketing (media) plans?'

- A few years after recovering from the dot-com bust, when my Contests2win business became profitable, I almost signed a joint venture agreement with a partner to replicate my Indian business model in Indonesia, Thailand, the Philippines and Singapore. The business, had I executed it, would have cost me tons of money and my precious time.

The flawed logic was 'where'.

Since none of these countries had an online contesting business in operation, I thought it would be a great idea to be the first to start in those markets.

I was lucky that the joint venture partner backed out. Later I understood that the 'where' didn't matter. The geographies and internet population at that time were so small that my business and its overheads would never have been successful.

I should have started with 'why' my business would have succeeded versus 'where'.

- Another classic failure happened when I applied 'what' as a starting point.

I launched an online press relations firm because none existed in the market. It failed.

There was no solid 'why' to make it succeed.

Thus, when I began plotting an entirely new business, I swore to ask why, why, why before anything else!

## Applying the 'why' principle

I sat quietly and began this conversation with myself:

Alok, why did your online branded contesting business Contests2win India do well?

Why did the mighty SoftBank (one of the world's largest and most successful internet investor groups) invite you to China to start the same business there?

Why did your online desktop contesting business so seamlessly migrate to a diametrically opposite mobile version and become even more successful?

Why did Walt Disney buy out your small business in China and make it their platform?

Why did the famous American Idol brand trust your small start-up Mobile2win with their franchise and give you the mandate to execute for them when they started in India?

Almost all these questions yielded these consistent answers:

- Each of these businesses made **games**.
- Games always attract **consumers**.
- **Brands** loved consumers and bought our services.

I continued my conversation with myself:

Why didn't all these businesses of yours scale and become household internet names? What restricted them? What forced you to sell out?

And magically, there was **one answer** to these questions.

Brands. Working directly with brands and clients and pandering to their needs.

Serving brands (to earn revenue) was the impediment, the stumbling block, the speed breaker. Brands never allowed me to test the boundaries of creativity and expression. Brands were selfish and close-minded. They demanded control and subservience. Being a servant of brands had been my Achilles heel.

As I contemplated this conversation, an image appeared in my mind.

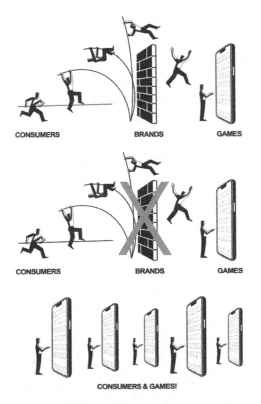

I impulsively asked myself, 'Why do brands matter? Consumers love fun games and now that I have the capital, the experience and the business model, why do I need to run after brands? If I can make games and directly engage consumers, I can WIN!'

This revelation was the genesis of my next start-up, Games2win—a mobile gaming company.

## LEARNINGS

- Never succumb to starting anything without thinking of the why first. It's the most painful of inquiries and yet the most meaningful. A pure, deep dive into the 'why' can save you from wasted effort, heartburn and regret.
- Always introspect. Many past events unfold their meanings and teachings over time. Learn from them as a continuous process!

# 3

# MDP—minimum *'dhandha'* product

The start-up world is familiar with a popular concept called the 'minimum viable product', aka MVP (popularized by the book *The Lean Startup*\*). Eric Ries, the author of the book and pioneer of the lean start-up movement, describes a minimum viable product as: '[the] version of a new product which allows a team to collect the maximum amount of validated learning about customers with the least effort.'

The concept of MVP helps you plan and launch a new product or service that is as basic as possible—with minimum frills and extras, using the least investment. The idea is to determine if the service or product is useful, and then build on it or ditch it.

---

\* Eric Ries, *The Lean Startup: How Today's Entrepreneurs Use Continuous Innovation to Create Radically Successful Businesses*, Crown Currency, 2011.

My version of the MVP is the minimum dhandha (business) product or MDP.

I have used it successfully to decide if I want to start a business or not.

## What is MDP? How does it work?

It's simple! After establishing the why, I examine three questions while evaluating a new venture:

1. Can this venture become a substantial business (achieve scale)?
2. Can I do this business differently versus others in the market (establish differentiation)?
3. Will this business earn plenty of profit?

If each of the three questions results in a strong 'yes', I consider starting that business.

To drive home how stringent this model is, only two of the hundred concepts I've put to the MDP test have come through as positive for me so far. That's a success rate of 2 per cent.

Let me share a real-life MDP case to explain this concept better.

After graduating in 1990, I worked in my father's socks factory for about eight years. The company (Hindustan Hosiery Industries) was an old, established business, and I had the opportunity to regularly meet many influential wholesalers, dealers and retailers from India's ready-made textile trade.

Three years after I had settled in, some traders began to urge me to start a ready-made jeans business as a new brand. Jeans were a new rage in India and were fast igniting the imagination of the youth.

While famous brands such as Levi's, Wrangler and Flying Machine served the higher end of the market, there was great demand for well-designed yet far less expensive brands. That was the opportunity (or at least an assumed one).

The traders sold me a vision—our socks company was well established and did regular business with the hosiery market, we had hundreds of authorized dealers across the country, we had been in business for over twenty years and had a solid reputation for making quality goods. So, adding a new business line of jeans would be easy and complement our ready-to-wear socks business. These folks even promised to order a large 'inaugural' shipment to prove their belief and commitment.

I calculated that a pair of jeans costs at least fifteen times more than a pair of socks, and if I could get this new business line started, then I would surpass my father's socks business turnover almost overnight!

As the traders' pitching gathered momentum, I decided to test the business case myself.

To make this a swift, efficient exercise, I promised to spend just a week to arrive at my verdict—should I launch the business of ready-to-wear jeans? I had to come to a clear yes or no.

I began in earnest on a Saturday morning and actioned my MDP methodology.

As step one, I got in touch with several small factories and processors who made jeans for small- to medium-sized brands as contractors. These were typical business-to-business (B2B) operators. They manufactured jeans for brands and also sold products under their own brand name. They agreed to meet with me.

I investigated the first question.

Can this become a large business (scale)?

The small manufacturers echoed what the traders had been telling me. 'Sir, with your brand and finances, you can do a large national business with jeans,' they said.

I moved to the second question of the MDP framework. Can I do this business differently versus the others in the market (differentiation)?

To get my answer, I drove to many of the factories and processing units of the manufacturers I had spoken to and studiously noted down what they were producing. I understood how shades, styles, different qualities of denim and treatments were being deployed to serve diverse consumer segments.

One aspect that caught my attention was the new rage of 'stone-washed' jeans. In large washing machines, jeans were washed with stones to give them the stone-washed feel, look and even occasional tear.

I was confident that I could innovate on the treatments and even thought of shooting holes through jeans and selling them as 'bullet-proof' jeans as a novel concept!

In a short time, the answer to my second question was, 'Yes, I could do this business uniquely versus the competition.'

All that remained was answering question three. Will this business make a profit?

Before visiting the different units, I bought a small pocket diary (the spiral-bound type that fits in a front shirt pocket). As I began touring, I wrote down the sales price of the different kinds of jeans each manufacturer was producing. The sales price was the net price after discounts, dealer commissions and returns.

As I visited factory after factory, I noted the cost of raw materials, labour, dyes, electricity, overheads etc., for each type of jeans being produced. I listed in my diary every unique unit I visited, with the sales price and associated costs of that product audited by myself.

After a long dreary day, I reached home, showered and was treated to a grand dinner. A while later, I whipped out my diary and began to deduct the costs of each of the jeans I had studied from their sales price that I had neatly noted.

I was shocked by my calculations. Most of the jeans I had studied barely earned a meagre five or seven per cent profit. Some, including the stone-washed range, lost money! I chuckled to myself when I thought about the cost of shooting bullets through jeans and how unprofitable that idea would have been!

Then why were these manufacturers still doing this business? I assumed the entrepreneurs had just resigned themselves to meagre profits and kept producing, hoping that 'things will get better' (a typical entrepreneur dream).

They might have started the business on an impulsive whim rather than a thorough analysis.

The answer to the third question in my MDP framework came swiftly: this was a perfect example of a hyped-up business with minimum or almost zero profitability. While the traders and intermediaries would make their margins, the manufacturer (which is what I was planning to become) would be the loser.

By the time I hit the bed, I had ditched the idea of being a jeans manufacturer. My MDP framework had done a fabulous job!

Fast forward a decade later to the question of starting a mobile games company.

When the idea of a pure gaming company crystallized, I had to use the MDP methodology.

Would MDP ratify my theory?

The only way to find out was to put it to the test, and that is what I did next.

---

## LEARNINGS

- Just because many people are doing a 'business' doesn't mean that the business is worth doing.

- Beware of people who encourage you to do work that suits them but not yourself. The traders who tried to influence me to get into the jeans business just wanted another '*bakra*' (sucker) to make money from.

- Be truthful to yourself. Don't let the excitement of an idea get the better of you. That's when most financial catastrophes happen.

# 4

## Patience is success

As tempting as it was for me to jump into executing my exciting vision of my gaming venture, I decided not to be impulsive. I had to test my idea as I did with the jeans business. I had to execute the MDP model and be convinced of the viability of the business idea.

As I thought through the process, I felt challenged. Unlike the jeans business that had been around for years in India before I decided to enter it, online gaming was completely new. I was a pioneer of this new format. There were no agents or contractors to meet and connect with. How would I start my MDP?

I started with a blank Word document and began to write down the standard three questions, starting with:

Can this venture become a substantial business (achieve scale)?

The answer to the first question of scale was obvious. Games have been popular since time immemorial. The Olympics are games, and millions of people watch them. The same can be said for cricket matches, *Kaun Banega Crorepati*, and even the occasional billiards game.

In the digital realm, once the Internet began to penetrate households and became affordable, online games exploded in popularity since they were so accessible and free versus the expensive 'console' games, which required significant investments.

The business of online gaming was massive. My first question of the MDP was ticked green!

I moved on to the second question:

Can I do this business uniquely and differently versus others in the market (establish differentiation)?

When I thought hard, I realized that my first start-up, Contests2win, WAS different. It enabled consumers to play branded online games, which had never been done before. So what was stopping me from innovating something new, again?

While it's tempting for entrepreneurs to hallucinate about their success, I had to validate my confidence or negate my overconfidence.

A critical development happened soon after.

In the eight years I had spent launching and running Contests2win, I had made hundreds of games for the world's best brands. These were driving games involving famous car brands, cricket games branded by top sponsors, dress-up games for fashion brands etc.

Each game we hosted also allowed consumers to win prizes sponsored by these global brands.

All these games had succeeded brilliantly, racking up thousands of responses.

As I thought about my new business opportunity, an epiphany struck me!

To test how these unique games would work as a new offering, all I needed to do was to remove the branding and then present the games to consumers stripped of the lure of prizes or a famous brand's endorsement.

And then, I had to determine if consumers were still interested in playing them.

What made this possible was my contracts and agreements with brands. I had made it legally clear that the games and the 'engines' (the way the game was played and programmed) that we had created belonged to my company. In contrast, the brands wholly owned their intellectual properties (IP), such as brand name, logos and branding elements. Once the promotion was over, the game would be removed from my site, and we were free to use our assets as we pleased.

Now when I contemplated starting a gaming website, I had the giddy realization that I already had hundreds of ready-to-launch games.

I turned to my trusted colleague Dinesh Gopalakrishnan (aka Dinu), amongst the first people I had hired in my first start-up. He had single-handedly produced most of the flash online games for Contests2win and java (a dated technology) games for Nokia handsets at Mobile2win. I gave him a list of specific titles and told him, 'Dinu, please remove the brands from these games and add them to a web portal.'

'What do I name the new portal?' Dinesh asked without raising further questions.

Impulsively came my answer, 'games2win.com, of course! After Contests2win and Mobile2win, why shouldn't we leverage our 2win brand and launch anything we do with a "2win"?'

This was how games2win.com, the brand, was born.

In three weeks, Dinesh did an incredible job of hosting almost fifty online games, stripped of the sponsoring brands, on games2win.com. We were live and good to go!

As I began testing our new games2win.com website and engaging with the content, the games struck me as odd.

A famous brand's driving game seemed meaningless without the original car as the prize to be won. Complex word puzzles initially sponsored by a Fortune 500 global coffee brand seemed banal without the brand logos and rich colours. A game that had to be completed in 'two minutes' (I guess you know who the sponsor was) made no sense when the two-minute brand was not omnipresent. I could spot similar deficiencies in almost all the games I played.

I was crestfallen and disappointed.

Later, I went back to the site and played some more games. I asked myself, 'Alok, while you created these games for global brands, how will new players visiting games2win.com know what these games were like originally? Why not keep an open mind, launch a trial website, and wait and watch what happens?'

I instructed Dinesh to make the website go live and prayed for success. I hoped and hoped that we would start getting organic traffic.

Barely any visitors came. It was a very slow trickle. For the next three weeks, games2win.com just 'existed', attracting between three to seven visitors daily via organic search results from google.com and top search portals.

I was unhappy. Maybe these stripped down versions of games were not ideal. Perhaps I should not even have tried this experiment, I lamented.

Hiding my disappointment, every morning I would gesture towards Dinesh, and he would reply to my signal by narrating the previous day's traffic numbers—'three', 'five', 'seven', etc. No more words were spoken.

These pathetic visitor numbers made me squirm each day.

I decided to wait for some more time.

Sometime in the fourth week, I casually asked Dinesh, 'How many visitors came yesterday?'

Dinesh smirked a bit and replied, 'Three seven.'

I got irritated and said, 'Dinesh, be clear! Three or seven?'

He smiled and said, 'Alok, thirty-seven! Somehow, thirty-seven people visited the site yesterday.'

I was shocked. Maybe there was a mistake in the numbers. Quickly, I logged into the Google Analytics dashboard to check the metrics for myself.

At that precise moment, over a hundred visitors were playing our games!

My heart stopped and then began to beat fast! A hundred concurrent users? How had this happened?

Then, understanding dawned. Search engines had taken three weeks to index our site, and now that games2win.com had been fully ingested by the search engines, visitors looking for online games were flocking to games2win.com!

Something seemed to be working.

I just hoped this was not a one-day freak incident.

As we basked in this new joy, an email came in via the 'feedback' section on the portal. It read, 'Hey, I like your website. The games are kinda corny but fun.'

I leapt with joy at being called 'corny'!

Another email soon followed. 'Can't you make more car games? Why should it only be driving on a straight road? How about curvy, twisty roads like the ones we see in real life?'

(How I wished I could email the sender and tell her that this was originally a branded car game, and the brief was to keep the road straight so the focus would be on the car. Sure we could make the most twisty road games ever!)

Now, I was excited and pumped up. Adrenalin rushed through my body.

It fast dawned on me that if I could make entertaining, original, cool (and corny) games, and with search engines hungry for unique content, a dream outcome was possible.

With hundreds of millions of new consumers discovering the free internet and searching for all kinds of things, including, of course, free online games, our site games2win.com would attract thousands of visitors.

In terms of business, this automatically meant that large audiences would trigger the potential to generate advertising opportunities on the site. Revenues could start rolling in.

The moment I thought of revenues, I immediately remembered question three of the MDP model. Will this business earn plenty of profit?

A disturbing doubt bubbled up. How would this business make profits?

The cost of making hundreds of games would be humongous. How would I manage this? As I thought harder, clarity emerged. The content of the game would determine our actual costs. If we made sticky, addictive games, which would remain relevant forever (think noughts and crosses), then costs could be contained. It was possible that with scaling revenue and almost fixed costs, I would profit from this venture.

Virtual products, especially games, have a fantastic advantage. Once made, there is no incremental cost to produce more units, apart from the minuscule cost of hosting and serving (bandwidth). And while the costs remain almost frozen, popular online games keep generating more incremental revenues as more and more players consume them.

This was the 'make once, profit forever' business model.

I gave myself a chest thump and reminded myself that if I could be innovative, this business of online games could work.

Circling back to the MDP, the answer to the third question in my MDP business framework, will this business make profits, seemed to be a yes.

As a logical next step, I launched Games2win as my next business venture and went all in.

## LEARNINGS

- I launched a skeletal, bad-looking website with games stripped of their poshness and polish to check if consumers would play such games. I chose to be imperfect to answer a perfectly relevant business question—would an online website of games stripped of brands and prizes work?

  Being 'perfect' is not essential in a start-up business, especially in the very early stages when you are testing hypotheses and prototypes. Frugality is king. Consumers savour newness and innovation and overlook imperfections that you may spot all the time.

- As a businessman or entrepreneur, whenever you create an original product, ensure you write agreements that protect and preserve your creations. If I had not had the clause that I owned the games and the engines I created for brands as my IP, I wouldn't have had a base to test games2win.com.

- Patience is the best friend of success. Never say never, and never give up. You never know how close you may be to the turning point.

5

# *Gabbar, Jaws, Yoda, Sasu Maa* and *Bahu*

With my mind made up to launch 'the best' online games portal in the world, I pondered on the next obvious question, which was, 'How does one **make** the best entertainment content in the world?'

The first industry that came to my mind was Bollywood. Bollywood epitomizes some of the best entertainment content created, at least in India. No sooner did I think of Bollywood than almost reflexively, the epic movie *Sholay* flashed in my mind as a reference. Polled multiple times as 'the best Indian movie ever made', *Sholay*'s scenes, dialogues and screenplay are legendary and remembered by most Indians. The movie is undoubtedly one of the defining moments in the evolution of Indian cinema.

As I meditated on what gave *Sholay* 'GOAT' (greatest of all time) status, I experienced a bolt of adrenalin! I had a *Sholay* connection. A memory of the movie buried in my mind suddenly bubbled up.

In the early 2000s, I was fortunate to produce and publish the first-ever mobile game for *Sholay* (via my previous company Mobile2win). At that time, the market was dominated by low-quality handsets, with Nokia phones being the most popular. The *Sholay* game we made was quite basic, with ordinary graphics and easy-to-play controls. It was more symbolic than a deep, engaging game. We all believed that *Sholay* deserved its own mobile game.

Given our innovation and first-mover advantage, the game attracted tons of PR, generated substantial downloads and was received well by gamers and the industry. It also generated meaningful revenue.

I clearly remembered that after the game had launched, I met Ramesh Sippy, the legendary director of the film. When I got a quiet moment with him, I asked him, 'Sir, how did you make *Sholay*? How did you even conceive it? What was the magical recipe you used to make the greatest Bollywood film ever made?'

As I waited with bated breath for his profound reply, Rameshji looked at me and burst out laughing.

He said, '*Arre baba*, if I knew the "formula", I would have made a hundred more *Sholay*s by now!'

I was stunned when I heard him confess that there was no secret sauce he had used to create such genius-level work. He made it out to be a stroke of incredible luck combined with hard work.

As I reflected on this incident, I refused to believe that the most incredible moviemakers in the world simply relied on good luck alone to produce timeless epics. Surely, they had a method, a magic wand that made everything turn to gold?

Maybe Ramesh Sippy got lucky with *Sholay*, but what about the other great directors?

I was buzzing with curiosity and began furiously researching the backgrounds of my favourite directors and producers—George Lucas, who created films such as *Star Wars* and *Indiana Jones*, and Steven Spielberg, who made *Jaws, ET* and *Jurassic Park*, amongst other great movies.

As I surfed, I stumbled across the story of the 'friendly bet' between these two accomplished men. I was amazed by what I read. As reported by *Business Insider*:

> A long time ago, on a film set far, far away, two directors made a friendly bet about a small space-fantasy film called *Star Wars*.
>
> Steven Spielberg would go on to win the bet and take millions of dollars from George Lucas over time.
>
> Here's how the out-of-this-world wager came to be.
>
> It all started with the troubles of 'The Star Wars'.
>
> In the mid-1970s, science fiction films weren't very popular.
>
> So when a young director named George Lucas tried to sell a script called 'The Star Wars' based on *Flash Gordon* space serials, few studios were eager to make it. It wasn't until Lucas took his script to 20th Century Fox that the film finally received backing—but even then, it was more because of the success of Lucas's previous film, *American Graffiti*.
>
> The challenges didn't stop there. A delayed, over-budget production caused Lucas to visit a friend shooting

his sci-fi film in Mobile, Alabama. That friend was Steven Spielberg, and the film being produced was his 1977 classic, *Close Encounters of the Third Kind*.

## The Bet

According to an interview with Spielberg for Turner Classics Movies, Lucas came to the set of *Close Encounters* out of sorts after problems with his passion project. Needing to recharge, Lucas spent a couple of days on set.

'George came back from *Star Wars* a nervous wreck,' Spielberg said. 'He didn't feel *Star Wars* came up to the vision he initially had. He felt he had just made this little kids' movie.'

After a few days, Lucas realized something else: Spielberg's *Close Encounters* would be much more successful than *Star Wars*. So much more that he felt like making a bet with Spielberg.

Spielberg would later say:

'He (Lucas) said, "Oh my God, your movie will be much more successful than *Star Wars*! This is gonna be the biggest hit of all time. I can't believe this set. I can't believe what you're getting, and oh my goodness. I'll tell you what. I'll trade some points with you. Do you want to trade some points? I'll give you 2.5 per cent of *Star Wars* if you give me 2.5 per cent of *Close Encounters*."

So Spielberg said, 'Sure, I'll gamble with that.'

*Close Encounters* would be a hit, making $303 million at the box office.

However, *Star Wars* would become one of the biggest box-office hits of all time.

According to Spielberg, Lucas sends him money from the bet to this day. Spielberg's gamble paid off—big time!

Released on 25 May 1977, on a budget of $11 million, *Star Wars*—later retitled *Star Wars, Episode IV: A New Hope*—went on to make $460 million in the US alone.

Adjusted for inflation, the film has made $1.48 billion at the box office, making it the second-biggest box-office hit of all time—only behind *Gone With The Wind*.

'*Close Encounters* was just a meagre success story. *Star Wars* was a phenomenon,' Spielberg said a few years ago. 'Of course, I was the happy beneficiary of a couple of net points from that movie, which I still see money on today.'

When I read this goosebumpy blog, a suffocating cloud of confusion lifted and left me with a vision of intense clarity.

I told myself, 'If the top content producers and directors of the world had no clue what they were making and the greatness they would achieve with their productions, it would be foolish for me to try and make "the best" games in the world.'

Movies pre-determined to be made as 'super-hits' were expensive to make, took inordinately long and had unpredictable success rates. The failure stories of such 'made for greatness' movies were painful to read. The financial losses of massive budget films such as *John Carter, The Lone Ranger, Mulan* etc.,* would make you cringe.

---

* Urquhart, Jeremy, '10 Big-Budget Box Office Flops, Ranked By The Amount of Money Lost', *Collider*, June 18, 2022, https://collider.com/10-big-budget-box-office-flops-ranked-by-the-amount-of-money-lost/.

So, I decided against the format. I was clear that I would not attempt to make complex, 'hit' games that could suffer the same fate as most movies.

Now, I had to plot an alternative creative strategy.

My mind wandered to the busy television industry, and my mom's fascination for Indian TV soap operas immediately came to mind. She regularly watched the '*saas-bahu*' (mother-in-law and daughter-in-law) sagas, romantic comedies and general entertainment shows that dominated prime television in India across channels such as Zee, Star TV and Sony Entertainment.

An intriguing question popped up in my mind, and I called my mom and asked her, 'Mom, tell me what happened last night in the saas-bahu TV serial you watch every day. What was the highlight?'

She was surprised by my sudden interest in content that I had earlier scorned and said, 'Alok, the saas and bahu made up for a while.'

I pressed further and asked, 'Cool. Now tell me what happened the day before and the day before that?'

Almost instantly came the answer I was hoping to hear. In a slightly irritated tone, my mom said, 'Munna (her pet name for me), I don't remember! I mean, who cares? I just tune in to these shows daily for entertainment and to enjoy some good time-pass.'

I thanked her and told her, 'You have no idea how valuable your answer is to me!'

Bolts of inspiration and profound business enlightenment struck me:

- Family dramas, comedies and crime serials on television were genres that never seemed to tire viewers.
- Each genre had shows with daily or frequent episodes.
- Some shows became super hits, while some faded away.
- As long as a TV channel had suitable genres and a few good shows, viewers would watch it daily.

I had nailed my creative direction. To replicate the business model for Games2win, this meant:

- I needed to identify the popular genres of games that I could focus on.
- I had to create individual games (like shows) within the popular genres.
- Like multiple episodes, I needed to make multiple games, a few of which would become popular, while most would fade away.
- As long as Gamse2win became an 'online channel' (like a TV channel) of entertaining and addictive gaming genres and games, gamers would come to our portal daily.

The general entertainment TV channel business would be the Games2win business playbook.

## LEARNINGS

- While we should wonder about outstanding achievements, never 'assume' how they were achieved. The 'how' may be completely different from what you believe happened. Instead, research, ask and find out how something was accomplished. The method may surprise you and make realize that you can do it too!
  This happened when I spoke to Mr Sippy and researched George Lucas and Steven Spielberg. In all, I probably spent less than an hour discovering the truth, but that simple effort paved the way for a direction I would spend years following.
- Develop an ability to join the dots. Understand different industries, spot patterns and then develop your insights from them. Nothing is ever written in plain words. It is always to be gleaned between the lines.

# 6

# The luckiest room-cleaning in the world

My wife Chhavi and I have two daughters. The younger one was born on the same day my first internet company was funded. The older one was born three years earlier.

Just about the time Games2win was launching, Chhavi decided to redecorate the 'kids'' room. After all, the girls weren't kids anymore. They already had expectations of what they wanted in their room.

As part of the process, all the stuff stored in the room, in its cupboards and lofts, was removed and placed in our living room for the impending 'keep or sell' decision.

As I walked past the large pile, I noticed a fascinating selection of dolls, doll houses and games that we had bought for our girls over the years. Next to the dolls and doll paraphernalia, I chanced upon my childhood collection of mini toy cars and comics (*Tintin, Amar Chitra Katha* and *Asterix*). I had refused to part with my toys and comics through the decades, even though Chhavi had pleaded with me several times. Now, they were with me again. My fondest childhood memories flooded my mind as I picked up the toy cars and lovingly held them.

As I opened the door of a tin car and spun its wheels, I experienced an electric eureka moment.

I was staring at dolls, cars and comics—an integral feature of every fortunate child's youth. I realized that despite the passage of time, these 'genres' of games had never become unpopular or stale. Even though I was the father of two girls, I realized how deeply I was still in love with my childhood toys!

Wasn't this fondness eternal? Car games, dolls and comics? Had I found the evergreen gaming genres I had hoped to discover at games2win.com?

Staring at the collections, it struck me that Mattel was one of the largest toy companies in the world, and it owned and sold Barbie dolls and Hot Wheels (toy cars).

What is the size and scale of Mattel as a business? I wondered.

Excitedly, I googled Mattel and landed on their corporate site. My heart began pounding as I read Mattel's financial statements:

- Net sales for 2007 (the year I did the research) were $5.97 billion, and net income for 2007 was $600 million!
- Almost 50 per cent of the revenue came from Barbie dolls and Hot Wheels franchises.

I took a few long deep breaths and began thinking of Mattel and the similarities with Games2win.

Mattel was founded in 1945. Barbie dolls appeared in 1959, and Hot Wheels debuted in 1968. We were now in 2007!

Even after almost fifty years, Barbie and Hot Wheels were doing solid business. These brands were generating billions of dollars in revenue, and that was a clear testimony that the 'genres' of dolls and cars were not just very popular but also immortal. Children spanning several generations had played with the same types of toys.

Post the arrival of the Internet in 1997, the playgrounds at home were changing. Everything was becoming digital. Toys and board games were fading away and giving way to digital entertainment. Kids' TV channels were popular, and YouTube was on track to become the largest entertainment destination for kids.

I pondered deeply and realized that if after withstanding ten years of severe disruption caused by the Internet, Mattel could generate Rs 25,000 crore in revenue and Rs 2400 crore in net profits *per year* (2007 rupee-dollar parity) via physical toys that were way past their prime, then a humungous opportunity was available in the digital world.

I was the person who would seize that opportunity. This would be my karma.

An intense clarity emerged in my mind about Games2win:

- I should create online games with the eternal, evergreen themes of dolls and cars, just like Mattel did with physical toys.
- Instead of physical toys, we would offer consumers a newer, fresher gaming format. I would migrate real-world toy themes to online games and entertain the world.

A bright, shimmering headline shone in front of my eyes:

'Games2win will pioneer doll- and car-themed games for casual online gaming and become the Mattel of the digital world.'

It was as straightforward as it could be.

---

### LEARNINGS

- Historic real-world successes can be great inspirations for launching New Age digital businesses if a common link or theme can be established. Sometimes, old is gold!
- Personal experiences can be one of the most potent and compelling starting points for building great ventures. What happens to us happens to others. So pay attention to everything around you. The most significant idea you may have may be inspired by your dusty attic or cleaning out your kids' room!

# 7

# A *kaali-peeli* (black and yellow) wins the race

'Games2win will pioneer doll- and car-themed games for casual online gaming and become the Mattel of the digital world' became my vision to kickstart Games2win.

In the world of gaming, the word 'casual' refers to a genre of games that have a few distinctive features, such as:

- They are easy to play (compared to, say, console games, which require complex learning).
- They are free for the consumer (versus paid games, such as console games).
- The art and graphics are of medium quality (versus the highly artistic PC and console games with cinematic art, sounds and special effects).
- They are packed with essential yet deep gameplay that impels the player to play repeatedly.

Old-world examples of casual games include Tic-Tac-Toe, Ludo, Snakes and Ladders etc.

I quietly assembled a small team from my previous companies to fire up the Games2win engines and was happy to see how excited they all were. My team and I had been involved in client service for years, and we were yearning to get started on building our own products.

I again turned to my colleague Dinesh Gopalakrishnan and decided he would be responsible for the car games vertical. My instructions to him were clear—'Dinu, you need to start making brand new parking and driving games. They need to be casual, differentiated and fun. Also, I need at least ten unique titles split equally between the two types. So, step on the pedal and hit the road now (pun intended)!'

Dinesh was excited and went all in.

Before mandating Dinesh to make casual car games, I had thought very hard about the genre. How could I make driving and parking games 'easy to play, but impossible to master' (the magical recipe for creating great games)? What would make these games sticky and addictive despite being casual and snacky (meant to be played for short periods)?

My insight came quickly.

Real-life driving was the best reference!

In the real world, we drive or travel in a car from Point A to Point B without colliding with vehicles, objects or pedestrians. It's impossible to imagine driving in the real world while having mini accidents on the way.

Leveraging this insight, I decided to build online car games with the opposite scenario. I wanted our online car games to be designed such that it would be impossible for a first-time player to navigate the car without an accident.

In the online game, while navigating congested roads and avoiding collisions with other vehicles, obstacles, pedestrians etc., players would not be able to complete a mission on the first attempt. After trying and losing the first time, the player would wish they had been more careful and would take another stab at playing the level.

Having bettered themselves, even if the player succeeded in winning the first level, the next level would be designed to ensure that a steep learning curve would be required to pass that level (play multiple times). The rest of the levels would gradually get harder and harder.

I was implementing the golden 'easy to play, impossible to master' game-level design mantra to make my first set of games.

Using this principle, a simple, well-designed game with minimum content could deliver multiple gameplays while providing endless entertainment to the player.

After understanding my design concept, Dinesh took up the task seriously and started game creation.

When we began thinking creatively for these car games, one exciting idea we devised together was a game called 'Bombay Taxi'. The idea's genesis was the streets of Mumbai. The ubiquitous black and yellow or kaali-peeli taxis, as they are fondly called, were unmissable and distinctly Mumbai.

If you haven't sat in a Mumbai taxi, you should bump it up to the top of your list of must-dos. The varied interiors, stickers, idols of gods of all religions perched in the centre of the dashboard, and the beads, malas and flowers dangling from every available hook in the front section will awe you. And at night, the interior lights and illuminations on offer can give the world's best designers a run for their money! Unsurprisingly, the first ever Apple store in India, which opened in 2023, is located in Mumbai and has drawn strong design inspiration from the inimitable kaali-peeli taxis!

Driving in Mumbai is hard. It means being super adept at navigating choking traffic, narrow roads, marriage, funeral and religious processions, avoiding crater-sized potholes, driving through flooded streets, zip-zapping two and three-wheelers and obeying all traffic rules and signals.

I often tell people, 'If you can drive a car in Mumbai, you can drive a car anywhere in the world!'

The reality of Mumbai driving became our game design, and Dinesh created different types of Bombay taxis (typically, older generation Fiat cars, small SUVs and mini cars) with distinctive stylizations. He designed terrific 'street levels' in Mumbai that featured fisherwomen selling their wares on the road, confusing railway crossings, kids playing cricket on the main streets, hawkers selling their wares almost everywhere, cows doing their own thing, food sellers, handcart pullers and the notorious 'three-wheeler' drivers, all contributing to the confusion and chaos that embodies the Maximum City .

Dinesh also amazingly recreated the sounds of Mumbai roads, featuring a cacophony of cars honking, hawkers shouting, trains, buses and trucks blowing their horns, street music and other typical Mumbai sounds.

The final car-driving game he produced was fantastic. The moment I started playing it, I couldn't stop. When I finally did, about forty minutes had passed!

Check out some of the *Bombay Taxi* images below.

No sooner did the game go live on games2win.com than it became a super hit! It was bound to be.

The idea and execution were brand new and had never been done before. Players who had been visiting our site were treated to a concept that was fresh, real, relevant and irresistibly addictive.

I was super happy and excited. We had published our first non-incentivized (without a prize) and non-branded (without a famous brand) game, and yet, the game was on fire! Players were already demanding more *Bombay Taxi* games.

When I reviewed the analytics of the game, I was stunned. Each level of the game was played between five and twelve times before it was completed successfully. My 'easy to play, impossible to master' recipe was working.

We had created not just a unique game but an immensely engaging one too. Players found the obstacles challenging and fun at the same time. With only twenty levels, the game delivered hundreds of gameplays per player.

Now, we had very early proof of success in our hands. All we needed was to add many more titles to our portal.

While all this excitement distracted me, a more profound, destiny-changing event was already in motion.

When I reflect on this, all I can say is that when you start doing new, innovative and enriching things, beautiful things begin to happen. Events, surprises and gifts you may never have dreamed of come your way.

What was transpiring unknown to me?

In our research on casual online games, Dinesh and I had come across three big websites that dominated this business. These were miniclip.com from the UK, addictinggames.com based in the US and Spil Games from the Netherlands. They operated sites such as girlsgogames.com, agame.com and others. These top sites featured various casual online games and attracted thousands of daily consumers.

Unlike Miniclip, the other two companies operated on a 'create and aggregate' business model, meaning they both made games and licensed games from other suppliers.

Dinesh had exchanged emails with these companies and was in regular touch with them, sending them updates on all our new and upcoming game releases.

A few weeks before publishing *Bombay Taxi*, Dinesh had casually asked me, 'Alok, since we are now making original games, can I send them to the top global game publishers for them to review and evaluate if they would like to publish our games?'

I remember being very distracted with work when Dinesh asked me this question. I even remember where I was sitting in the office. Without giving it much thought and not even bothering to look at Dinesh, I mumbled, 'Sure, go ahead'.

So, Dinesh sent our brand-new *Bombay Taxi* to these companies.

Addictinggames.com (at that time owned by Viacom), the largest online gaming website in the US, immediately replied that they wanted to try hosting the game on their site. They added that if it did well for a few days, they would return to Dinesh with commercials on how the arrangement between our companies could work.

Without further checking with me, Dinesh wrote back to them with a 'Sure, go ahead' message.

My absent-minded 'go ahead' that led Dinesh to approach global aggregators would change the course, destiny and future of Games2win forever.

When I think deeply about it, if I had applied my mind, I would have told Dinesh to 'hold on' and NOT send the game to anyone. After all, I wanted to be a destination for online games, not a games supplier.

But as we have, no doubt, all experienced in our lives, destiny and Lady Luck have their unique ways of manifesting themselves. As the famous saying goes, 'No one, not all the armies of the world, can stop an idea whose time has come'.

Games2win's time had come. In less than a year, the world's top gaming websites would be demanding our games, and we would have the product power to entertain the whole world.

## LEARNINGS

- Some of the best inspirations are right now, within your grasp. Just like *Bombay Taxi* was for Games2win. You don't have to travel to exotic places to find inspiration. Just be open-minded to your environment.
- Creativity can sometimes be a trap. Beyond an 'idea', an entrepreneur should think deeply through the business model. I had a clear vision of how car games would be a powerful business engine for Games2win and then embarked on creative output. I propose you have a business model parallel to cultivating a creative vision.
- Good things have a way of finding their moment of glory. Just keep innovating and doing your best. Many other things will happen on their own!

# 8

# Distribution or revenue—what comes first?

Addictinggames.com (AG) hosted our *Bombay Taxi* game on their site, and it was a smash hit! They had taken a great call by experimenting with an unknown company (Games2win) and an unfamiliar product (*Bombay Taxi*) and had taken our crazy and funny game to US audiences—the most demanding and competitive users in the world. They loved our game!

This particular success was my sweet spot. From the day I conceived Games2win I was obsessed with finding success in the global market.

**There were three whys:**

1. The past decades of software exports that had created the Infosys and TCSs of India were focused on services (providing clients with solutions).

   I wanted to prove that India could make software products worthy of global standards. Successful products create gigantic companies of a global scale (Microsoft, Google).

2. The stark difference in monetization between India and other markets. For example, if 1000 players in the US playing one of our games watch one ad each, I stand to earn $10. If 1000 players do the same in India, I barely make $1. The difference is 10x.

3. Profitability. The only way a gaming business that was heavily dependent on advertising revenues would become profitable would be if the business generated its revenue from top Western countries versus India. India was a great place to make games, not sell them. My formula was to create costs in India and generate sales in the US.

My goal was crystal clear: Games2win would make games *from* India *for* the world.

Given the acceptability of our local game *Bombay Taxi* in the US market via our distribution partner addinctinggames. com, I had found my highway to drive into the Western world!

All I needed to do was repeat *Bombay Taxi*'s success many times over and this time using global, relevant and creative themes.

As luck would have it, AG needed online games. Lots and lots of them. Launched a few years before games2win.com, the site had become the number one destination in the US for teens and tweens who loved playing casual, snacky games.

The massive success of AG came with its own set of challenges for the company. Since it served millions of consumers every month, AG couldn't keep up with creating enough games to satisfy the ever-ravenous youth who visited the site several times a day. The AG payers expected new games to be published on the site as often as possible.

AG needed to find partners who could supply it with as many games as possible, and by pure luck and providence, it had found Games2win (or let me say, we had found them).

After *Bombay Taxi*'s surprise success, AG wrote to Dinesh inquiring about our capacity to supply them with online games on an ongoing basis. They were interested in hosting as many of our new games as possible as we met their quality requirements.

Dinesh introduced me to the AG business team, and I took over the discussion.

Before responding to the question of capacity, I reviewed the addictinggames.com site thoroughly. The website published between twenty to twenty-five new games a week, mainly in car driving, parking, dress-up, puzzles etc.

What quickly caught my attention was the diversity of these games. Most of them were not manufactured by AG, and many of them had a unique look. A majority of the games were far inferior in quality I had expected to be on Viacom's website.

This convinced me that lots of these games were sourced by AG from partners such as us, and many of these partners were amateurs, small studios or one-man shops. Almost all these game suppliers had no website of their own. They made games only for licensing to the large portals. They were the quintessential 'indie' developers or independent developers.

As I played many of the games on the AG site, what intrigued me was the lack of branding, logos or company names of those who had supplied these games. I realized that AG probably paid these independent developers a small licensing fee to use their games on the AG portal or simply bought their games for a fixed fee.

Given that AG wanted to work with us actively, we could monetize all the new games we planned to produce by driving a hard bargain with AG. We were a large company and not a small game supplier that had little bargaining power. This would generate a new source of revenue for Games2win—something we had never planned for in the first place.

As I pondered this new source of potential revenue, I felt something was amiss. I thought I was returning to my services model of charging clients fixed fees. This was a new business! I had started Games2win to escape the wrath of clients.

There had to be a bigger prize to be unveiled. I needed to dig deeper.

I checked the statistics of the AG website (via tools like alexa.com) and was stunned to find that the site attracted almost ten million visitors from the US. The US was (and is) the most lucrative market for gaming (ads rates, paying users) in the world. While games2win.com was now attracting about a thousand visitors a day globally, we had very few visitors from the US.

As I compared the Games2win US traffic numbers with those of AG, I was hit by inspiration. It was a eureka moment that would once again change the destiny of Games2win.

I decided that I wanted to be paid in 'traffic' through a barter system rather than receive a few dollars in licensing fees.

I had built my first start-up, contests2win.com, using the same media barter model. My first and big success had come with India's MTV for whom I created online contests in exchange for free advertising of my online portal on the MTV channel. It was a win-win. MTV India got free online contests and my website got free TV promotions.

Now, it was time to replicate the same in the most valuable market in the world.

As discussions progressed between our companies, I introduced the barter idea to AG. Then, things went into a higher orbit. The vice president of the company got involved and aggressively tried to convince me to stick to their licensing model (fees, no branding) versus what I was demanding.

I stuck to my ask and did not yield.

Internally, Dinesh and the AG team members were chatting as usual. The AG team had noticed how frequently Games2win was creating and publishing new games, with clockwork timing. We had begun with one new game a week, then scaled to two, later three and were soon hitting anywhere from four to five new games per week. Almost all these games were global and would work well on the AG site.

The AG team recognized this and kept telling Dinesh they 'hoped to see our new games on the AG site soon'.

This back channel confirmed what I knew—AG was hungry and would yield to my demand.

The vice president chose to play the old fashioned 'who blinks first' business game with me. He stopped responding after a couple of email exchanges. I went into an even deeper freeze.

'Who blinks first' is a business art form. When you want something and ask for it, do not get impatient or restless and give in. Staying quiet or not communicating with the person you are negotiating with is a challenging but highly effective method of negotiating. The person who blinks first (writes or calls back) is the person who gives in.

In this battle of wits, I would not be that person.

A few weeks later, the vice president of AG wrote back asking, 'If we were to agree to brand your games, what would be the terms?'

When I read that email, I smiled and applied my training gained over the years. I would leave nothing to chance or ambiguity.

I sent back a detailed presentation with a mock game clarifying what we wanted from AG in exchange for them hosting our weekly games.

We asked for:

- A clickable logo of games2win.com that was a live link to our website and was always present as the 'right ear' (top right-hand side) of our games.
- A guarantee that our branding would always be visible if the game remained hosted on the AG sites.

Armed with a working prototype, images and PowerPoint presentation, there was nothing left to chance in my reply. I hit send and waited.

The days rolled by without any reply from AG.

I kept my cool and bided my time.

A couple of weeks later, the vice president replied, 'We've discussed this at the management level and are, in principle, okay with your proposal. Let's convert this into an agreement and start rolling.'

The morning I read that email, I knew something magical and unmeasurable had been set in motion for Games2win. My intuition would be proved right, and how!

## LEARNINGS

- When an opportunity comes by, don't just jump at it and accept what's being offered. It may have several more layers of rewards to be unpacked. You just need to have patience and a curious state of mind. Take your time in accepting deals.
- Develop market intelligence to help you make better decisions. Relying only on your gut and feelings is rudimentary. The more you know, the better your decisions will be.
- Never blink first in a negotiation game, especially when you don't have much to lose but a lot to win. It's an unnerving discipline but fabulously rewarding.

# 9

# Looking for a CTO and finding a spouse

Chhavi and I had been married for sixteen years when I launched Games2win. I was all set in my life-partner department.

What I needed badly was an incredible tech partner to complement me (I'm a BCom graduate with a good grasp on finance and accounting).

At Games2win, the business plan was to build and publish consumer-facing online games. I needed a solid, experienced chief technology officer (CTO) to own and execute the company's technology needs.

I asked the tech folks I knew for recommendations and mandated a headhunter to help me.

A few weeks later, I received an email with a resume and a recommendation for 'Mahesh Khambadkone'. He seemed to have solid experience in gaming, which included console games and setting up significant infrastructure technologies for casinos and betting companies. He had studied and worked in the UK and the US. He was based in Bengaluru.

A quick conversation later, Mahesh, aka 'MK', was in my office for a face-to-face meeting.

I instantly connected with MK. I liked him. He was soft-spoken, gentle and cared to listen more than talk. He was the opposite of my personality. He reminded me of Chhavi!

After discussing my plans for Games2win and understanding the idea I had for scaling online games, MK asked me about the tech stack we had in the company. He wanted to understand how the servers, back-end etc. were set up.

I cautioned him that I was the business guy and didn't know much about tech but would try my best to explain our set-up. For questions I didn't have answers to, I would say, 'That's why I need someone like you.' He quickly understood my predicament.

Towards the afternoon, MK asked, 'Alok, where are the UPSes? I want to understand their capacity.'

I had never heard the word UPS before. Well, I had heard of UPS as United Parcel Service—the global courier company—but I knew MK wasn't talking about them.

I looked bewildered and asked, 'What are UPSes? What kind of machines are those?'

MK seemed a bit frazzled and said, 'Power backup systems. I want to see them.'

I shook my head in ignorance and called a couple of folks in the IT department (which has become the number you call when *anything* doesn't work, irrespective of whether it's even related to what they do). IT said they had never heard of the word UPS before.

I was nervous. I didn't want to look like a fool in front of MK. I probed and asked, 'MK, what do these machines do? What is their purpose?'

MK said, 'Whenever the main electric power supply goes off, the UPS machines kick in and provide power so the electricity supply in the office (or home) is uninterrupted. UPS stands for uninterrupted power supply.'

I burst out laughing and told MK, 'Oh my gosh. Now I understand! MK, this is South Mumbai. We never have power failures. We've never needed UPSes. That's why I couldn't relate to the question or the problem.'

What I had said was a fact. Thanks to Tata Power and BEST (Brihanmumbai Electricity Supply and Transport), companies and consumers on the small island of South Mumbai had enjoyed uninterrupted power supply for the fifty years that I had been staying here.

This UPS incident was a bread-breaking moment for me and MK.

We laughed in surprise. Instantly, MK and I knew we would be working together. Even towards the end of our meeting, he never inquired about his compensation or employee stock ownership plan (ESOP) or financial rewards. I instinctively understood that MK was a purist. He loved technology, ideas and challenges. He wasn't an opportunistic or greedy techie interested in massive pay hikes.

Later that week, I proposed that I travel to Bengaluru and spend some time with MK, hang out in his office and meet his boss, the founder of the company that created back-end infrastructure for gaming companies. My idea was to be transparent with MK's boss and tell him about our possible collaboration. Maybe Games2win could partner with his current company? This would be a positive approach to help him adjust to the fact that MK might leave him to join Games2win rather than him finding out abruptly one day.

The day before I flew to Bengaluru, I asked MK to choose a lunch spot for our meeting. I wanted to observe how my future partner and CTO would engage. Would he prefer a costly five-star hotel and make lunch a grand affair? Or if he invited me to his favourite restaurant, I wondered what that place would be. These were my standard tricks of 'KYO'— know your chief experience officer (CXO)!

MK suggested we meet at Ballal Residency for lunch.

In all my trips to Bengaluru, I had never heard of this place.

When I reached Ballal, it looked like a slightly upgraded Udipi restaurant in Mumbai.

The lunchroom was more like a college cafeteria, with no air conditioners. I spotted waiters who looked like they were from the 1960s, sporting uniforms that seemed to be from the Hindi movies of yesteryears.

The setting amused me. It was new for me!

When we finally met and sat down, I asked MK about his choice. He said, 'It's a hundred metres from my office and an old classic establishment in Bengaluru. It serves pure veg food—(I'm a strict vegetarian). I thought it would be a good spot for our meeting and the subsequent visit to my office.'

I smiled.

MK's personality was quickly revealing itself. He was practical, not ostentatious, frugal and straightforward. I liked that a lot.

Post my return to Mumbai, I meditated on the next steps. MK was my partner in the making. Unfortunately, my past partners had ditched me when they were offered more money or left me during downturns. This time I wanted to ensure MK was 'the' right partner I was looking for.

So, I thought of two situations that would test his commitment to Games2win and help me determine whether he was thinking of it as just another job.

The first one was an unorthodox proposition.

I had been in discussions with a large gaming company in South Korea for an exclusive licensing deal for one of their games for India. This was a complex, MMORPG (massive multiplayer online role-playing game) that was a complicated, high-tech project, unlike the simple casual online games I was publishing on games2win.com. MMORPGs were unheard of in India and their chance of success was unknown.

I proposed that MK travel with me to South Korea to meet the company I was trying to partner with.

My terms for MK were tricky. If the MMORPG deal worked out, then I would be happy to write out an employment contract with him. But if the deal went sideways or failed to materialize, then I wouldn't hire him.

This was certainly not a regular job proposition for someone who could be the CTO of the company. How could one deal be the deciding factor? That too of a product and technology that was alien to India. It seemed silly and juvenile, and unprofessional.

Tech leadership roles in India have always commanded a high salary premium, combined with extra 'scarcity' compensation. My proposal was the antithesis of cajoling, coaxing and bribing a super techie to join a fledgling start-up!

But, MK replied, 'Sure, let's do it.'

The second ask was a tougher one.

If things were to progress and we were to work together, I proposed that MK move to Mumbai for at least the next five to seven years to build Games2win with me.

MK had recently married, and his entire family was based in Bengaluru and Mangaluru. After spending many years abroad, he was finally settling in Bengaluru and would frequently travel to Mangaluru. I assumed that since he would also be planning to start a family soon, the Bengaluru-Mangaluru arrangement would work wonderfully given MK's local family support.

And here I was, an unknown guy asking him to come to a hostile, angry city like Mumbai and work for an extended period, disrupting his present and future lifestyle.

Mk replied, 'Sure, I'd be happy to.'

I had major goosebumps. This person wanted Games2win to WIN and to be a partner in its success—not just an employee.

Circa 2023.

It's been sixteen years since I met MK, and we are co-founders of Games2win.

I joke that I was looking for a CTO and found my second spouse. I firmly believe that co-founders and spouses are the same.

In the process, I've also learned that there is one test that infallibly checks if you have found a co-founder or not.

I call it the co-founders blind test.

How does it work? It's simple:

Place two or more potential co-founders in separate rooms and ask them questions ranging from ethics, conduct and morals to best practices and first principles.

## Examples:

If you get a chance to sell this company for hundreds of millions by overstating its capabilities, would you?

If your VCs were being unjust and punishing you financially for no reason, would you compensate yourself via the company's cash in unauthorized ways?

If you wrongly hire a person for a job that doesn't exist and then have to let them go, will you tell them the truth?

If a salesperson leaves the job after a year and has sales commissions due to them for deals they closed before their last day of employment, would you pay them the money due?

The test is how each candidate answers each of these questions.

If the replies are 100 per cent identical (even a 99.99 per cent score is a fail) to yours, then you have found a co-founder. Else, it's better to think of that person as an employee.

## LEARNINGS

- While choosing co-founders, be hard on yourself and the other person while clarifying expectations. Ask the most uncomfortable questions and be prepared for a negative result if it doesn't work out. Maybe that is a better outcome for you in the long run.
- There is something more significant than ambitions, expectations, goals, wins, losses, exits, acquisitions, IPOs and bankruptcies. It is your values. And the litmus test of co-founders is that they have identical values.

# 10

# Laxmi loves to play hide-and-seek

I have a time-tested belief—money comes when you least need it, not when you most want it. So, take it when it comes.

The successful exits of my previous companies, Mobile2win China and Mobile2win India, had yielded a large payout for my parent company Contests2win, which owned substantial shares in both these companies. After paying healthy dividends to the Contests2win shareholders, I had plenty of money left in the bank to start new ventures.

I proposed to launch games2win.com as a 100 per cent-owned business division of the parent company, and my board approved this. At that time, we loaned $1 million (about Rs 4.5 crores) to Games2win. The money was to be used by me to start and scale Games2win.

Since I was fully funded at the start of the business, I didn't need to meet potential investors. But, I have always valued the input of venture capitalists, who provided me with much more value than just cash in my previous companies. VCs were my mentors, knowledge sources and sages of wisdom, given their vast experience across a portfolio of companies. They also opened doors and introduced me to contacts, relationships and businesses worldwide.

As a digital entrepreneur in this New Age business domain in India, I was frequently invited to conferences and seminars. So, when I was asked to be a speaker and panellist at an Indian gaming conference at the Indian School of Business (ISB), Hyderabad and saw a couple of venture capitalists as my co-panellists, I immediately accepted the invitation.

Being a start-up entrepreneur who had almost perished in the dot-com bust, I had trained myself to be frugal. That meant maximizing every rupee spent and extending the 'paisa vasool' concept to everything I did.

Take, for instance, travelling to different cities for work. I followed a self-imposed diktat called 'first in, last out', meaning I would always take the first flight into a city and the last one back. How was this *paisa vasool*? Well, it was a simple hack to maximize time in the town I was travelling to so that I could do more business.

The only time I broke my own rule was in this current instance when I had to travel to Hyderabad for the conference at ISB.

I cannot remember why I didn't book the first flight and chose to go on the second one. On reaching Mumbai airport, I discovered that my flight had been delayed. As I did the maths in my head, I realized that I would probably not make it in time for the panel discussion. It made no sense for me to travel.

Embarrassed by my foolishness and miscalculation, I called my wife and said, 'Chhavi, my flight is very late. I made a mistake not taking the earlier one, so I'm considering returning to the office.'

What Chhavi said surprised me. She said, 'Alok, you stepped out of the house to go to work, so do your work and come back. There is no returning midway.' She disconnected the phone. Chhavi had never said something like that to me before. It seemed she was telling me to go to Hyderabad even though it was illogical. Or maybe she was subtly telling me that I should have followed my travel rules, and since I had disobeyed myself, I needed to learn a lesson.

Whatever motivated her to speak those words, I took the flight and reached the ISB campus a few minutes after my panel discussion was supposed to have begun. Luckily for me, as it often happens, the earlier programmes were running late, so I was able to make it to my session on time. The discussion was about entrepreneurship, and when I was introduced to the room, I was applauded.

The two recent exits of Mobile2win China and India had made me a little famous.

As the discussion began, I looked out for the venture capitalists who were my fellow panel members.

Immediately, I noticed a distinguished young man in an expensive designer jacket. He looked like a male model from Raymond's 'Complete Man' campaign or straight out of GQ magazine.

He spoke slowly, with measured words and an air of authority. I quickly scanned his name placard and discovered he was Rahul Khanna from Clearstone Venture Partners.

I had neither heard of Rahul nor his firm. But what he said next got my attention.

In an authoritative tone, Rahul described the tremendous opportunity in online gaming and how India would mimic China, where millions of consumers played massive multiplayer online games (MMOG) in plush internet cafés. The gaming companies that had launched these businesses in China had become multi-billion dollar ventures and had been listed on the local stock exchanges.

Rahul then quoted numbers, demographics, user preferences and other triggers that would fire up gaming in India, as it had in China.

As I listened to him, my heart began to thump faster. Here was a VC talking about my domain! I was the guy who had pioneered gaming in India, and what Rahul was so eloquently speaking about was my space. Even as my ego took a beating, my mind raced. As an entrepreneur, I knew that if a VC was diving deep into a domain, they would likely finance it or announce a deal soon.

As all kinds of fears crossed my mind, I felt my phone vibrate.

When I quietly peeked at it, I saw an SMS from Ganesh Rengaswamy, who was sitting in the audience. Ganesh worked at Greylock Partners—a prominent global VC fund—and was responsible for its Indian business.

Ganesh and I knew each other well. Ganesh's message confirmed my deepest fears. It read, 'Alok, it seems Rahul will announce a gaming deal very soon. Better watch out, my friend, your space is getting competition.'

I hung on to every word that Rahul said, bracing myself for the funding announcement of a local gaming company. Oddly, no such information came. Rahul concluded his presentation by commenting on how India could become one of the most significant opportunities for internet gaming in the world.

When the panel session ended, I met Rahul and introduced myself. He had heard of me. As we chatted, I was happy to learn that he was a South Mumbai lad like me. Before I left the ISB campus, I promised to meet Rahul in Mumbai soon.

What transpired in the weeks that followed was nothing short of magic.

Almost every week I visited the plush, elegant Clearstone office on the seventeenth floor of the Oberoi Towers, with a majestic view of the Arabian Sea. Like an emperor, Rahul sat at the single desk that occupied his office suite and quizzed me on the future of gaming and how I thought the Indian market would evolve. While I had a conservative approach, I shared Rahul's bullishness about the Internet and its potential in India. Since I had already launched Games2win that was all about consumer gaming and excitedly shared my plans with Rahul. My vision for Games2win was a global, casual gaming business built out of India for the world.

As our meetings intensified, Rahul and I discussed the details of a 'go-to-market' plan for Games2win. I introduced Rahul to MK. Rahul seemed convinced that Games2win had the team and execution plan to be a winning business.

However, I did not agree with his belief that India would mimic China in consumer gaming. Nonetheless, we decided to review that piece of the business in greater detail if we agreed to work together.

As unbelievable as it may sound, in less than three months, Clearstone prepared a term sheet for the company to invest about $4 million in Games2win, which had barely started up six months ago!

A month later, as soon as all the complicated documents were signed, Rs 18 crore landed in my company's bank account.

I was now funded to scale Games2win with more capital than I had planned or imagined.

Even more unbelievable was that Clearstone preferred that the original $1 million I had loaned Games2win from my holding company be returned! They didn't want Games2win to have any debt on its books, and their Rs 18 crore in funding was more than sufficient to repay the Rs 4.5 crore I had borrowed from my own company.

In all my past experiences of raising capital, funding businesses, and even selling two companies, I had never seen a deal close this fast. The speed and the frictionless connection between me, Rahul and Clearstone was surreal. The transaction seemed propelled by factors that went beyond the ordinary. It was as if an invisible force was behind it, determined to make it happen. (The other side of this story is captured in my second book *The Cave*.)

---

* Alok Kejriwal, *The Cave: An Internet Entrepreneur's Spiritual Journey*, Penguin Ananda, 2022.

The day after the deal was inked, I said to Rahul, 'When you made that speech at ISB, I thought you would announce a deal that day. Were you planning to?'

Rahul gave me his classic grin and said, 'Yes, I was going to announce a deal. I had written out a term sheet for Kreeda Games [another Indian gaming company] the night before I flew out, and the promoter and I had agreed that I would announce the deal at the ISB summit.

'That morning, when I landed in Hyderabad and switched on my phone, I saw a message from the company promoter that he was not interested in my offer. The deal was off. So, I had a speech but no deal!'

Kreeda Games did raise money from IDG Ventures, SoftBank China and India Holdings a few months later but could not pivot its business and had to shut down its operations three years later.*

Fate and destiny had played a remarkable role in securing funds for Games2win even when we didn't need them. A lot more would transpire thanks to this fantastic partnership with Clearstone.

---

* Cherian, Jacob, 'Two VCs Invest in Kreeda', *Economic Times*, June 12, 2007, https://economictimes.indiatimes.com/industry/media/entertainment/two-vcs-invest-in-kreeda/articleshow/2118581.cms?from=mdr.

## LEARNINGS

- You must make it a point to keep meeting people. Magic happens when people meet. For years, I followed the practice of meeting two new people daily. I have learned that every conversation you have is a learning experience.
- Serendipity or luck happens when you least expect it but when you are always trying. In a *Time* magazine article I read when I was ten years old, the top fifty CEOs of America were asked to share what made them successful. The most common answer was 'to keep dealing'.
- When starting a company with your own money, always write out a loan to it rather than investing in it as equity. Loans are meant to be returned (as it happened in my case when Clearstone preferred I return the money I had borrowed from the parent company). Equity is meant to be invested forever, which means your money is tied up for a long time.

# 11

# The most successful failure ever

When Clearstone funded Games2win, it came linked with an investment hypothesis that 'India will mimic China' in online gaming and consumer behaviour. To leverage that insight, I was expected to implement a super successful gaming business that existed in China but was as yet unavailable in India.

'India will mimic China' was the 'flavour of the decade' for innumerable VCs. For ambitious entrepreneurs, the hack was straightforward. If you could do something involving the internet and mobile phones that was successful in China and presented it in a well-crafted PowerPoint as a plan, you could quickly raise a few million dollars from investors just to try out your idea!

When Rahul Khanna of Clearstone mentioned the same view (at the ISB conference), I refused to buy into the logic. But since my Rs 18-crore investment came to Games2win with this condition, I agreed to give it my best shot.

Why was I sceptical of the 'India will mimic China' narrative?

For one, I had started, built and sold an internet start-up in China (Mobile2win acquired by Disney) and knew that market. It was the opposite of the Indian market. Some of the dissimilarities between India and China were outright alarming and worrisome.

Consider daily life and the political situation.

In China, the State plays a dominant role in the lives of its citizens and controls a large part of the day-to-day lives of Chinese nationals.

For instance, during my time in China, we couldn't organize simple office parties without police permission. Every time the team went out, we had to get a permit from the local police station to allow it! This was due to the rule that any 'gathering' larger than an X number of people needed permission.

In another case, a dear office colleague born and raised in Shanghai began dating a man from Beijing. When they decided to marry, she needed to get approval from the police or some department for this inter-city alliance! Further, the movement of citizens within China was strictly regulated, and they weren't allowed travel freely throughout the country (as we have in India).

Media was strictly controlled, and we had to watch what we said, shared and joked about in that country.

Keeping this practical experience in mind, I knew that copying Chinese gaming formats would not be a successful bet.

But conversely, I had also learned on multiple occasions that being close-minded was never a good idea for an entrepreneur, especially for an internet one! VCs knew markets, understood trends, could bet on outcomes, and even put their money on the line. Why forego the chance of things working out by not giving it my best effort?

What were the unique characteristics of the Chinese gaming market?

As I dove deeper into it, I learned that a particular gaming format that had succeeded beyond imagination was the MMORPG business.

Millions of Chinese youth would huddle in cellar-like cybercafes and spend hours playing complex online games and competing with each other, partnering with friends (as gangs, clans and guilds). While the games were free, these young players would constantly pay for small items within the games, such as weapons, clothes for their avatars, superpowers, collectables and special abilities.

The payments were micro-sized (between Rs 10 and Rs 50) but made frequently. The result was a massive revenue for the gaming companies, which kept growing year after year as players went deeper into their favourite games, which were rich in art and graphics and updated regularly.

The most popular genre of such MMORPGs was mystical battles, featuring human and non-human characters and creatures battling for land, treasures, victories and spoils while travelling across mythical lands.

To make it easy for you to imagine, think of the *Lord of the Rings* movies, packaged as a continuous online game played by millions of players over many years.

When I tried to play some of these games, I failed miserably. The characters seemed alien to me, and even the enemies were dragons and flying demons that I could not relate to. Most of these games were based on mythological stories from Korea and China and had no commonality with our Indian heritage. My reference, for instance, was the classic and immortal Ramayana—the ultimate source of innumerable stories, battles, gods, demons, superpowers, fantastical weapons, animals and creatures, all melded into one amazing, epic tale. Where would I get a Ramayana in China?

I needed a game format or genre that would be instantly relatable to people in India.

While meditating on this challenge, I thought back on which of our games had enjoyed significant success in India. Instantly I remembered *Bombay Taxi*—the car driving and parking game, which was a massive hit in India (and had even tasted global acclaim).

Logically, I asked myself, 'Why not look for a car driving and parking game with MMORPG elements that we can introduce in India?'

Searching the Internet for car-based MMORPGs in China, I was amazed by what I found.

A game called 'CT Racer' had decent success in China and Korea and was manufactured by Hyundai and SEGA—the legendary Japanese gaming company).

Excitedly, I sent an enquiry via the CT Racer website, introducing myself and my plans for India, crossed my fingers and waited for a response.

The very next day I received a warm, positive email from the CT Racer team, who were more than happy to explore a partnership for launching CT Racer in India.

One discussion led to another, and MK and I were soon on a plane to Seoul to meet the CT Racer team and try and close a deal.

The CT Racer game seemed to be the perfect match for India. It was all about driving cars, racing against online opponents, or cruising with friends 'going for drives'. It even had a taxi mode in it!

The 'city' in CT Racer was an amalgam of Shanghai and Seoul and looked zippy and cool. This signalled that the company knew how to create life-like digital cities well and if needed, could add Mumbai and Delhi maps to the game.

Thousands of Indian teens played car racing console games such as *Need for Speed* and *Grand Theft Auto*. Following that logic, the game should do well in India.

After a couple of months of discussions, we had negotiated a deal.

Games2win would license CT Racer exclusively for India, deploy it across Indian cities and cybercafes and sell in-game merchandise (cars, avatars and accessories) to players. If the game was a hit, SEGA and Hyundai would model Mumbai and Delhi and create a unique 'CT Racer India' game for Games2win.

In terms of costs, I negotiated hard and got away with paying $400,000 (Rs 1.8 crore) as a fixed licence fee for the first three years and a small revenue-sharing agreement on revenues earned as royalties.

While the fixed licence fee seemed large, when I did my diligence on MMORPGs, I found that the licensing costs of most top games were in the multi-million dollar range per country. I was in no mood to blow up half or even more of my funding just procuring a licence for a game format with no precedence of success in India. I was glad I was paying only 10 per cent ($400,000) of the $4 million I had raised as fees for a game that was 'as perfect as it could be to deploy in India'.

Three months later, we were ready to go.

I went all out in trying to make the game a grand success.

I told myself I had to give this game and business line my best shot. I hired a cybercafe team that began to visit the top ten cybercafes in the top ten internet-penetrated cities in India (around 2008–10, cybercafes were quite popular in India's top metros and satellite cities). I visited at least half of these cybercafes myself.

While deploying the game in these cafes, a scary incident occurred. To embed the game in the PCs of the cybercafes, we asked the CT Racer team for compact discs (CDs) of the title so we could use them to copy and transfer the multi-gigabyte (GB) game quickly. These CDs could also be distributed freely to players who wanted to play the game from home. Instead of encouraging piracy, we thought of providing free CDs with attractive packaging and details to fire up game usage.

The Korean team replied and asked, 'What is a CD?'

I was taken aback and assumed a CD must be called something else in Korea. So I explained what it was, sent some pictures and hoped it would explain the ask.

Quickly, their reply came: 'Sorry, Mr Alok. This storage format was used many years ago in Korea. We don't even use DVDs now for contents (the Koreans always use the plural 'contents') distribution. Now, we only use the Internet. The

CT Racer game of 4 to 5 GB gets transferred to a cybercafe PC within a few minutes. It's the best and safest way to distribute original IP.'

I was shocked. I didn't have an internet connection of that quality at home or in the office, so it was highly unlikely that any of the hole-in-the-wall Indian cybercafes, whose main business was providing email and web-surfing services at that time, would have one. An uncomfortable thought pricked me. What else would I discover about this game that would be difficult to replicate in India?

Shrugging off this problem, we copied the game ourselves on CDs and began business!

To make the game seem busy and populated, we hired game jockeys to sit and play the game all day in shifts. While pretending to be players, these jockeys would engage the real players in the game, challenge them to races and make friends with them. I asked half the game jockeys to use girls' names so as to get the teen boys playing even more interested. Not surprisingly, most 'girl' jockeys got all the attention and friend requests.

For the in-game items such as cars, petrol, avatars, car decorations etc., I began with minimum pricing. I compared India's and China's purchasing power parity (check the Big Mac Index) and priced the items far lower than what the formula showed. My idea was to generate massive adoption and popularity of the CT Racer title. Since the game was free, all players needed to do was pay for cybercafe time. The time spent in the cafes generated revenues for the owners, who then pushed the game via posters and messages to their regular customers. The hope was that the CT Racer game would increase the time spent by customers in the cafes and thus deliver more revenue to the owners. This would be a real win-win.

We did everything possible, but the game failed to generate interest among the Indian audience.

Out of desperation, I came up with a scheme whereby cybercafe owners wouldn't charge CT Racer players for café time and Games2win would compensate the owners for the revenue thus lost. Now, with the game free to play and even free to access, I hoped that the Indian youth would begin to play in droves. I wanted to do everything possible to get the game in front of Indian internet players.

When we offered this incentive, the player numbers picked up, but the moment we stopped offering free cybercafe time, the numbers would drop sharply. This meant the players were not genuinely interested in playing the game. I didn't want to make incentivization a permanent plan. It was like paying consumers to watch a movie. The game was not naturally interesting.

After three months, the game remained a disaster. We were hosting barely a thousand players a day while incurring massive operating costs to service cybercafes, manage operations and pay the salaries of the jockeys. What made the maths worse was that even the daily thousand-odd players rarely bought anything in the game. They just wanted to drive around and chat with our game jockeys with girls' names!

While I was deeply disappointed, I also felt vindicated. My intuitive feeling about this game genre had come true. MMORPG was not meant for India. 'Works in China' did not mean 'will work in India'.

Games2win was not alone in its muck-up with MMORPG. When we were launching, a competitor called Kreeda Games (the same company that Rahul Khanna had written out a term sheet for) launched an exciting dance-based MMORPG called *Dance Mela*.

It was a unique song and dance game. Players had to choose an avatar and make them dance and compete with other players. There were even special 'dancing mats' that the players could dance on, connected to their computers.

Top Bollywood choreographers had been hired to create unique Indian dance moves to make the game relatable. Famous models and celebrities launched this game with much fanfare.

The *Dance Mela* game was an even bigger failure than our *CT Racer* game.

The greater tragedy was that Kreeda had staked their entire funding on this one game, creating deep Indian content and extensive marketing. Just as the game crashed, the company went into a terrible financial crunch. It eventually shut down a few years later. The collapse of Kreeda was ample proof that MMORPGs were a massive flop in India.

So, why did these global hit games (such as *CT Racer* and *Dance Mela*) fail domestically?

The reasons were eye-opening!

## The climate

Most of India has a tropical climate throughout the year. So young Indians tend to spend a lot of time outdoors whenever they can.

It is the opposite in China and Korea. These countries are frigid for large parts of the year. The cybercafes are warm and snug and people thus enjoy spending time in them. Sure enough, once inside a cybercafe, MMORPGs become the preferred mode of entertainment.

## Family

Indian parents (at least back then) are very involved in the activities of their children, to the point of over-policing and micromanaging them. 'Gaming is bad' is a proclamation I've been hearing for years now. Parents want their children to study and happily spend lakhs of rupees on tuition fees and study courses but refuse to pay even small sums for their kids' cybercafe time.

In Korea and China, parents of teens are open to giving money for cybercafe time. It is acceptable to hang out with friends and game, and stay safely indoors.

## Choices of entertainment

In India, we have cricket, Bollywood (and many other kinds of 'woods'), hundreds of television channels, malls, parks and various other sources of entertainment. If nothing else, we play gully cricket on our streets.

So why would young Indians spend time in cramped, dark, stuffy cybercafes to entertain themselves when they have so many alternatives?

In China, entertainment is strictly state-controlled. Movies, television and all media are heavily censored.

MMORPGs were mildly regulated by the government (at that time) and therefore became one of the best avenues for youth entertainment.

In Korea and China, gaming has become a cultural habit, like playing cricket in India. That is what led to the massive success of MMORPG titles in those markets.

What eventually happened with our game?

Nine months after I launched *CT Racer* in India, I decided to shut it down and exit the MMORPG business completely.

## LEARNINGS

- I de-risked relying heavily on a single business idea, which I was not sure of and that could have sunk my company if it were unsuccessful. I've always proposed and championed starting slow, learning fast and then ramping up or down a business vertical based on its financial success. I call the MMORPG project 'the most successful failure'.

- Investors want the best for their investee companies and the entrepreneurs they back. This does not mean that they are the best judge of the business that these companies should do. Entrepreneurs should have the clarity and ability to separate financial discussions from business engagement when investors are involved. Suggestions from investors are always welcome. Diktats to operate the business in a particular way are not.

- Nothing is proven until tested. I am sure that one day there will be a massive MMORPG success in India, despite all the odds and challenges I have mentioned. But timing is critical and lethal. While being at the right place at the right time and with the right idea is rare, it is common to be in the wrong place at the wrong time and with the wrong idea. That's the curse entrepreneurs should beware of.

# 12

# Everything gets stolen

As planned, Games2win was on track to become the Mattel of the online games space with fresh and innovative car driving and dress-up games.

From our launch date, along with driving and parking games, we were global pioneers in dress-up games. Barbie was my evergreen inspiration, and Games2win was the first to introduce life-like models with a narrative and deep storyline for our players.

I had closely observed my daughters play make-believe games with their dolls. So, also, in our dress-up games, imaginary 'customers' presented the players with demanding missions and projects to execute, with specific fashion requirements. Players loved our games for the complete immersion we gave them in fashion. Many commented that they had improved their fashion sense after playing our games.

In addition to regular fashion, we introduced wedding styling, make-up and haute couture games to offer our players a complete experience in the dress-up realm.

To produce these games, we were probably one of the first companies in the world to hire real-world fashion designers, stylists, make-up artists and hair stylists to create virtual content. My vision was to operate in the same manner that global fashion businesses like Zara and H&M operated—except that we were virtual, not physical!

Our car games, too, began to explode in popularity. My team and I created several concepts around cars that included bus driving, airport driving simulations, and taxi and valet parking games. As we deepened our understanding of this domain, we stumbled upon a gold mine—teaching teenagers driving rules and road signs, which would help them get driving licenses later and then drive cars in the real world.

We were 'gamifying' driving and all the challenges that came with it.

As these games began to get published, games2win.com quickly became popular on the internet. A significant advantage we had (in addition to our site) was the global distribution partnerships with Addicting Games (Viacom US) and Spil Games (Europe). Both partners were the most prominent online gaming sites in the world and were liberally licensing our games on a traffic-for-content barter business model. All our original titles on these global sites had live links to our website, and that drove crazy traffic to us.

Games2win.com began picking up crazy momentum in visitors. In less than a year, we ramped up from a few hundred visitors a day to many thousands and began approaching the hundred thousand daily mark. I started dreaming of the day when we would achieve one million visitors a day.

Then suddenly, it all went dark. Something broke. It was as if someone had flipped a switch and stopped traffic coming to our site.

Daily visitor count, which had been galloping at breakneck speed, began to wind down. Traffic began decreasing day by day, and we had no clue why.

After a detailed audit of servers, technology implementations and website hygiene, we could not find anything amiss. Our Google search rankings had significantly improved. When I typed 'free dress-up games' on Google, the first or second link would be a Games2win game. Ditto for the car games.

Then where was our traffic? Why had players stopped coming to the site? What had happened?

I had an idea. Instead of searching for 'dress-up games' and 'car games', I typed the game titles, such as '*Bombay Taxi* game' and 'best friends forever dress-up', to see what showed up. When I hit enter and saw the results, I nearly fainted.

With the massive global exposure that our international partners Addicting Games and Spil Games had given us, internet pirates had discovered our games and website. They had stolen all our games.

How was this possible? The reason was the technology we were using.

All our online games were made using Adobe's Flash software. It was the most popular tool (or framework) to make online games that worked within a browser. The technology was outstanding and adaptive to all our artistic and monetization requirements.

However, Flash has a significant flaw. On any website, flash games could easily be 'right-clicked' and saved to a computer or laptop. These downloaded files (SWFs) could then be directly uploaded to another site and made ready to be deployed. Simply put, anyone could play games made in Flash on any website, download them, upload them on their site and launch their own business!

Shockingly, copying a fully developed, complex game was as simple as clicking, downloading, saving and uploading.

Our entire library of online games was available for immediate piracy. And global pirates had done a phenomenal job of stealing everything we had made so far!

To understand the extent of the damage, I once again queried '*Bombay Taxi* game' on Google. Instantly, I saw hundreds of links bearing the name of our game. Unfortunately, most of the top links pointed to unknown, amateur pirate sites that had stolen our game, created new pages of our content and placed ads around it. We had lost not just our traffic but revenue as well. (You can google '*Bombay Taxi* online game' and find these pirated sites hosting our game even today or scan this code.)

With a heavy heart, I searched for our top twenty games and noticed that all of them had been stolen and copied infinite times. Some of these pirates were so good at their job that when I searched for specific games, the pirate sites appeared above the link to our website. Not only were the pirates adept at stealing our IP, but they were also better than us in web search engine optimisation (SEO).

As I slumped in my chair, a harsh realization hit me.

Our online games business would never create value given this new menace.

Since traffic had begun plummeting, our only source of revenue—advertising—had started to decrease sharply. At the same time, we had invested significantly in hiring people and creating production facilities with costly hardware and software. The cost of making games had increased, and now the revenue per game was collapsing.

This was a horrific lose-lose situation.

If we wanted to stay afloat and make Games2win a real business, we would have to tackle these pirates first.

## LEARNINGS

- Success is never upwards and linear. It is always punctuated by deep cuts and lows that make you feel demolished and defeated. Those are truly the moments that will test your character and conviction and your will to plod on. Never stop at the lowest points in your life. A magnificent high awaits you.

- Most precious things get stolen, copied or pilfered. This includes business models, intellectual property, and even team members you train, groom and cultivate. If you are the creator and lose some important assets, understand that you will create even better ones as replacements. Creators can't get stolen— only their creations.

# 13

# Engine fail

Clearstone was my lead investor in Games2win, and the business was headed by Rahul Khanna in India. Post our chance meeting at ISB, Rahul and I had developed a fantastic relationship working together, which only accelerated after the first round of investment. Given his experience working with product companies in the US market, he was instrumental in helping me think of Games2win as a products business versus the service business mindset I had acquired while running my previous ventures.

Rahul reported to Sumant Mandal, a Clearstone partner based in Santa Monica, California.

Sumant and I had interacted over short, formal, sporadic video calls. I knew Sumant was a fantastic investor who had funded some legendary start-ups in the Bay Area, and I yearned to engage with him on a deeper level for Games2win.

As it usually happens, when you want something sincerely, you receive it.

I got my opportunity to meet Sumant when he visited India to meet the Clearstone portfolio of companies, which included the now legendary BillDesk. Our meeting was also marked as a formal Games2win board meeting so we could conduct our statutory business requirements and welcome Sumant as a Games2win director.

As the board meeting approached, I began to work hard on the Games2win business presentation for my board members.

As I started populating the deck, the slides and the content on them began to make me nervous.

First, our MMORPG business had failed. There had been little organic interest from Indian players in CT Racer. When we offered cash prizes and free internet cafe time, there would be some uptick in engagement, but once the incentives were withdrawn, the usage would come crashing down. I knew this was an unsustainable business model for driving engagement and usage. I had stopped it quickly.

I had pinned my hopes on our online business of car and dress-up games being the main engine of our growth and success. The business had demonstrated strong consumer traction, and our global distribution partnerships were helping to scale our traffic in leaps and bounds. Sadly, a few weeks before the first board meeting, piracy had struck this business in a massive way, and it was in steep decline.

Every slide I added seemed shallow, insignificant and fake.

I was crestfallen. This was the first official board meeting of Games2win, and I had nothing substantial to present. If we had no business left at Games2win, what would the board meeting be about? I wondered.

The next day, I gathered my courage and conviction about my business and shrugged off the dismay and gloom that had overcome me. To make my presentation slick, I added slides of our new online games, pictures of the best-looking cybercafes in which we had introduced *CT Racer* and data and metrics of our online games, attractively represented on a global digital map with heat spots (red for the busiest cities, orange for medium traffic etc.).

I added many slides on the new employees we had hired and how the organization was growing.

But no matter how many slides I added, in my heart of hearts, the presentation seemed feeble. It was more like the sales pitches I would make to impress clients in my earlier ventures.

Only gas, no mass.

The day of the board meeting arrived, and Sumant Mandal and Rahul Khanna from Clearstone, Ash Lilani from Silicon Venture Bank (SVB had participated in the first round with a minor investment) and a couple of folks from Nexus Capital all assembled in our medium-sized conference room.

Sumant was very warm, friendly and encouraging and led the meeting. His personality shone through when he entered our office, and he seemed to be in complete control. My first impression of him was that he appeared very noble—a quality I had never seen in VCs.

After a few minutes of pleasantries, Sumant looked at me and asked, 'Alok, how is the business going, my friend? Rahul tells me that you are up to some great things at Games2win.'

My throat went dry. I tried to gulp but couldn't. I returned a half smile and softly said, 'Sumant, let me present a deck with updates.'

Sumant gestured for me to stop and said, 'Don't worry about a presentation. Just talk to us. Tell us what is happening.'

My stoic composure gave way, and I felt exposed and vulnerable. My PowerPoint was no longer a prop I could lean on. A second later, I told myself, 'Alok, these are your partners. Just like MK, these are folks who will ride the entire journey with you. Don't hold back. Be yourself and speak the truth!'

My opening sentence was a line that I will always remember. I said, 'Sumant, we had a great business, but it has disappeared. Now, all we are left with are funds but no business.'

Sumant heard these words and chuckled. He was so relaxed and calm as if my words had not bothered him. For those few seconds, my mind froze. I was unable to read him.

Sumant requested that I explain the situation in detail, and I did just that. I explained how the MMORPG business was a dead duck, and the online Flash games were being stolen left, right and centre.

Sumant was keen to know more about Kreeda Games, our competitor who had also launched an MMORPG, *Dance Mela*, which was being advertised heavily and was quite visible in Mumbai. Maybe Sumant had also spotted those ads?

Rahul Khanna had seen the *Dance Mela* ads plastered behind Mumbai's BEST buses and was quite upset that I was not advertising *CT Racer* with similar aggression. I had gently explained to Rahul that folks who drove cars and saw an MMORPG ad on the back of city buses were not the target audience of such games. It may have made some sense to advertise *Dance Mela* on the back of buses, but certainly not *CT Racer*.

I brought up this matter in the meeting. I wanted my investors to understand my philosophy of marketing and advertising. I shared that I was not a fan of advertising or marketing digital products. The world's greatest digital brands that had become household names were rarely advertised. I couldn't remember seeing ads for Instagram, Google and WhatsApp when they launched. I further explained that in the case of *CT Racer*, it made more sense to advertise an MMORPG in the environment where it was played—inside a cybercafe or near cybercafes and colleges where the target audience hung out.

I gave the board the grim reality of *Dance Mela*. It was doing worse than *CT Racer*, despite the crores of rupees that had been invested in customizing the product for India and then aggressively advertising it. The Indian teen boys who typically played MMORPGs weren't getting excited about playing a dancing game on a PC.

Dance-based MMORPGs appealed more to girls and did well across China and Korea, considering the large number of girls that thronged cybercafes and didn't play aggressive slaying, shooting or racing games. When we were launching MMORPGs, there were barely any Indian women gamers in the market.

In India, *Dance Mela* had failed even before it had seriously started as a business.

Sumant listened carefully and then became a bit reflective.

He said, 'Alok, what do you want to do? Shut down the *CT Racer* game?'

This wasn't a trick question. It was more of an encouraging suggestion to coax me to open up and speak my mind.

Nonetheless, I was shocked to hear Sumant even suggest this because MMORPGs and their business implementation in India were why Clearstone had funded me in the first place! How could I take the money and then opt out of the execution of the business plan?

My mind cleared. This was my moment of truth, and I remembered one of the first principles I had adopted while starting this venture. Neti, neti—to decide what not to do at all costs.

'Yes, Sumant,' I replied. 'I want to wind down this business division ASAP.'

Sumant grinned and said, 'Alok, this is YOUR business, and you will decide what to do and what not to. We are just your partners to support you along the way.'

That was my second 'bread-breaking' moment at Games2win.

Sumant was a genuine partner. He was there for the long haul. Like MK, he was genuinely invested in the business beyond just writing out investment cheques.

After the years of bullying I had experienced from previous investors across my earlier ventures, this simple, straightforward clarity sounded like divinity speaking.

I told the board I would decide on the MMROPG and update them all.

As regards the online games and games2win.com and the acute case of piracy, Sumant was incredibly upbeat about what we had achieved. He said, 'The fact that you have created products that are being played worldwide without any marketing is a magical feat. Don't worry; you'll figure something out.'

The meeting concluded with formal requirements, and the rest of the investors left the office. Rahul and Sumant stayed back, met the team, walked around the office and absorbed the atmosphere and energy.

Sumant invited MK and I for dinner that evening, and left the office saying, 'Alok, what an amazing start! We're going to have a lot of fun together.'

I was trembling with gratitude, excitement and relief. How could this have happened? I had been expecting the worst, even a scenario that had the investors asking me to liquidate the company and distribute the funds left.

This was a magical board meeting of a kind I had never experienced before.

(Readers may be interested in reading the chapter 'All's Well That Ends Well' in my book *Why I Stopped Wearing My Socks*, which chronicles a board meeting from hell that was diametrically opposite to what I experienced at Games2win that day.)

## LEARNINGS

- Never dress up (pun intended) the truth! Every business has many dark corners and ugly moments. As the owner, you must first shine the light on the awful news rather than pretending to be in a place where you are not.
- Investors can break or make a start-up. And they are not easy to find. In earlier blogs, I've written about VC being an acronym for 'vulture capital', 'vampire capital' and 'vapour capital' as well as venture capital. In the case of Clearstone, I had found a VC firm that could be termed as providing 'value' capital. This investor was interested in creating value for the business versus just returns for themselves. The highest quality in the VC order!
- Being truthful about concepts, beliefs and opinions, however difficult, is very important. Suppressing your ideology in the presence of your investors is a bad idea. Your silence will be misconstrued as agreement or, worse, acceptable action.

# 14

# The magic of Inviziads—our visible, invisible ad!

The week after our first board meeting, MK and I sat in our conference room, shattered and distraught.

Day after day, by the hour, pirates were stealing all our online games and publishing them across hundreds of sites. For these dishonest operators, even a few dollars a day via advertising revenue was meaningful. For us at Games2win, it meant the death of our business.

As we mulled over the problem, my training in meditation and spiritual practices began to kick in. There are five fundamental principles we imbibe in our training and learn to use as we live our real-world lives.

The first principle is that 'opposite values are complementary', which I felt was apt for the situation we were in.

What was complementary about getting our precious games stolen?

When I removed the veil of negativity in my mind, quite a few positives popped up!

For the first time (thanks to the pirates), our games were being exposed to millions of players across almost all the countries in the world—a feat we had never thought would be possible. While our global distribution partners, Addicting Games and Spil, attracted substantial US and European traffic, these pirates were publishing our games in Asia, South America and even countries in Africa!

So, the first win was that we had more 'distribution'.

As I thought more about this, a profound thought struck me.

I asked myself, 'Why do people steal things? And what do they steal?'

The answer was obvious: Anything that is stolen has some value. No one steals the garbage off the streets and takes it home.

So, what is valuable gets stolen. And that value is then used by robbers for personal gain.

It simply meant that our online games were quite valuable. That was why pirates were stealing them and publishing them on their websites. This also meant they were incurring the costs of operating those sites. So if they continued to steal our games and publish them, then no doubt they were still making money, which reconfirmed that our games were embedded with lots of value.

When this occurred to me, I sharply reminded myself I was not in a Sunday meditation class listening to smooth sermons. Logic aside, the trauma of seeing my business evaporate before my eyes was tough to bear.

As MK and I grappled with the problem, we consulted technocrats, entrepreneurs, lawyers and experienced professionals who had created amazing IP and had dealt with the menace of IP theft. Tons of advice came rolling in. Threaten to sue each site! Create a template of a legal notice (a cease and desist) and keep sending it to all the websites you identify as pirates. Most websites will get scared and stop hosting the game/s.

(A cease and desist notice means 'stop and discontinue'. It is a very effective way of tackling piracy or any intellectual property violation on the internet.)

Deep down, I knew this was a costly and futile exercise. The pirates, by nature, were robbers and untraceable. And if they did not pull the games down, what could we do? How on earth would we sue hundreds of thousands of sites across numerous countries?

Someone else strongly suggested creating digital rights management software or DRM. This was advanced software to protect content, such as our games, using complex code and protocols. A good DRM would stop our games from being played on unauthorized sites and also cause the game to self-destruct.

Again, I knew this was the wrong choice. DRM software was very restrictive, and pirates and hackers could crack anything. If we released a version of DRM software, pirates would tackle it, and we would have to update and release a newer version. We would spend our time creating and updating anti-piracy tools rather than making more games!

I retired to a closed conference room and closed my eyes. I recalled my second spiritual principle, which was to 'accept people and situations as they are'.

I thought hard . . . how could I accept thieves and their activities? What value were they adding for me? I was no saint to accept sinners with mercy! I was a fully funded entrepreneur who had to ruthlessly and aggressively create value for his business.

But I persisted in contemplating this principle.

Suddenly, a violent shiver ran down my spine.

What if, somehow, we could *leverage* the act of piracy versus fighting it? What if we made these so-called thieves our 'frenemies'?

After all, the pirates were doing an incredible job of distributing and popularizing our games beyond our wildest imagination and abilities.

We just needed to do something to complement their effort. There was some switch somewhere that needed to be flipped.

I thought harder. Why were these pirates stealing our games? What was their benefit? (My 'why before who, when, where and what' principle kicked in.)

In a flash came the insight—the pirates used the stolen games to create an internet game page and placed ads in the open areas of the page. These ads generated money for them. And since we were creating new games each week, the pirates had found an incredible supply of content to steal and upload on their portals.

As I thought of the 'why', a thunderbolt of inspiration struck me. What if we could include ads *inside* our games, when they were on pirate sites? Then we could earn money from our games even though they were on websites they were not meant to be on. Even if traffic was not coming to our site due to pirates, at least we would make the revenue we were losing.

A little explanation: we had ads on our site, but those ads were not part of the games. They were a layer on top. So, when the games got stolen, the ads would be left behind.

My pulse began to race. I thought, if I were a pirate and stole a game that showed ads inside the game, I would not steal it. It would be a put-off. As a pirate, I would want to publish ad-free games and only my ads around the game, on the sides.

At that instant, I had a Newtonian epiphany. Forget an apple, an insight the size of a watermelon dropped on my head! I had a major eureka moment.

What would happen if the ads inside the games remained invisible when the game was available on official sites (like our own and our partners), but after the game was stolen, the ads would become visible after a few hours?

The challenge was to create ads that could remain invisible and visible, depending on where our games were hosted.

What was the benefit of these ads remaining invisible and then becoming visible?

It was straightforward. When stealing our games, the pirates would not see these in-game ads because they were invisible. After lifting the game and placing it on their site, the ad would become visible a few hours later (so they would not be noticed immediately).

This concept of invisible ads becoming visible led to the creation of 'Inviziads' by MK.

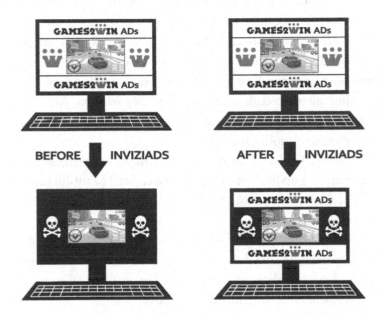

MK took over the implementation, and within a few days, had the solution ready.

We added Inviziads to all our new and old games and waited with bated breath as they were uploaded.

A few hours later, early results began to stream in.

They were magical!

We saw a massive surge of ads that began to generate impressions worldwide.

The numbers were incredible! Starting with a few thousand a day, we saw Inviziad impressions skyrocket to one million, then five million and settle at ten million impressions monthly.

Assuming that our games were played by unique players once or twice, the numbers meant that we now served over five million new players each month across all the top global markets.

In effect, this doubled Games2win's audience reach and opened up tremendous growth and monetization ideas.

Just after executing this massive deployment, MK and I took a step back and once again did the most contrarian thing anyone could imagine.

Instead of placing commercial ads in the Inviziads stream (and making up the lost revenue), we created beautiful brand ads of Games2win that would appear wherever an Inviziad was fired up.

The ads we had placed inside our games were friendly and cheerful. In our dress-up games, the Inviziad's message was, 'Do you like playing dress-up games? Come to games2win.com for hundreds more!' Similar messages were created for the other genres of games.

Why did we do this?

I wanted to claw back traffic to games2win.com and immerse the new users from the pirate sites in the great catalogue of games we had on our leading portal.

I knew that if a player came once to games2win.com, they would be hooked and return repeatedly. That was a substantial and positive outcome for us, versus earning a few cents per ad. Long-term returning customers were infinitely more valuable than one-time buyers.

The call we took worked, and how! We saw an almost new set of one million unique visitors rushing to our site, which eventually settled at seven million. We had added 70 per cent of new visitors just by leveraging the power of piracy.

In addition, more magic began to appear at the backend of Inviziads.

Instantly, we could track every city and country where our games were being played. We were astonished at our reach. We had penetrated over 100 countries and served games across thousands of cities.

Unplanned by us, Games2win had silently created an online ad network that could serve ads in any country an advertiser wanted.

While we did not commercialize Inviziads, there was a real, tangible monetizable benefit that we could now quantify. Very few (I did not know of any) global gaming websites owned their own private ad network.

Games2win had its own Inviziads!

As this business began to scale, we kept improvising on how we leveraged this innovation:

- Pirates became our best friends. On our site, we added messages such as: 'Please feel free to copy this game and use it on your site', knowing very well that for each visitor we lost, we would get ten back through Inviziads.
- Our game producers and their game quality were now measured by how often their game got stolen. The bigger the Inviziads count of their game, the more superior it was deemed to be because pirates only stole what was the most valuable.
- We patented Inviziads, a cornerstone of our Games2win online games business.

Unknowingly, Inviziads would also become the magical fortune teller of Games2win in the near future.

When I reflected on this saga, it was thrilling to realize that pirates and their acts of piracy, which seemed to be the biggest curse for us, had turned into our biggest boon!

The crowning moment of glory in this entire episode was informing Sumant and Rahul of the dramatic turn of events at Games2win and how Inviziads were now driving the growth of the business that I had proclaimed 'dead' in the last board meeting.

I still remember the one line reply I received from Sumant in response to my celebratory mail. It read, 'I told you, you will figure it out.'

## LEARNINGS

- There is enormous potential that can be unearthed from the worst of events, situations and circumstances. You must have the calmness of mind and positive attitude to discover and unleash it. (I strongly recommend learning and practising meditation to cultivate contrarian and innovative thinking.)
- Business happens when there is a win-win. When you think of how you can win while benefiting the other person as well, magic happens. We didn't block the pirates or call them bad names on their sites via our ads. We won, and they won.
- Old, traditional and conventional thinking can become a millstone around your neck. You must break out of the shackles of one-track mindsets and develop a 'how do I leverage this negative situation' mindset that challenges everything before accepting it.

# 15

# A humbling lesson in greatness

As Inviziads began to buzz and create a global footprint, we learned of an innovative company called Mochi Media that was implementing a similar solution, not for itself but for other online gaming companies.

Mochi Media was based in San Francisco, and their solution, MochiAds, did not have the 'invisible becomes visible' feature. It was an ad solution for online games that could not be ripped out by pirates and would remain visible all the time. Mochi monetized MochiAds via advertisers and kept a certain percentage of the sales as their commission.

MK and I wanted to learn more about their business and how we could commercialize Inviziads at a later stage.

My agenda was to snoop around, ask the Mochi management as many questions as I could and secretly build on the knowledge gained for Inviziads.

It was a short-term, selfish and secretive way of thinking that I had seen all around me while doing business in India.

The 'smart' operators would hold their cards tightly to their chest, get as much information as possible from the competition and then use the knowledge gained to beat everyone. Their principle was to 'take everything and give nothing'.

We travelled to San Francisco and connected with Mochi Media. I requested a meeting with their top management, which was readily accepted.

This pleased me immensely. I understood that Games2win was now a recognized entity in the online gaming business in the US, and I would now get access to the 'secret sauce' that was making Mochi Media so successful.

The CEO and founder of Mochi Media, Jameson Hsu, met MK and me warmly. After settling down in his cosy conference room, we began our discussions. I kept shooting questions about MochiAds, going deep into distribution practices, their rate cards and pricing, business metrics and performance parameters.

Jameson spoke freely and answered all my questions. After almost forty minutes of my quizzing, Jameson gently asked, 'Alok, how are Inviziads doing? I see you guys have gone live with it. Congratulations!'

I was stunned. My throat went dry, and my face must have revealed my deep embarrassment. I was sitting in front of someone who knew exactly what I was up to and the competitive threat I came with, yet had so graciously entertained all my questions with smiles and warmth!

I meekly replied that Inviziads had started well, and we were only hosting 'house' (our own) ads to claw traffic back to our site.

Then, Jameson dropped a bombshell and said something that shocked me.

He said, 'Alok, you guys are so bright. You should be based in the Valley.'

I half-heartedly mumbled, 'Jameson, I wouldn't know where to start. We've always operated from India and only travel occasionally to the US.'

He immediately replied, 'You can start right here, in our office. Occupy a couple of desks, and you can make your plans later.'

I experienced a shiver down my spine when Jameson made that offer. In that moment, I understood why Silicon Valley succeeded the way it did. The people who made Silicon Valley what it was, gave, shared and spared whatever they had, no holds barred.

And in my case, Jameson knew that I could use his knowledge against his company, yet he invited me to sit in his office.

Why did Mochi Media and its CEO even make this bizarre offer? (Think of it—would you ever make such an offer to your slimy competitor?)

The reason was simple. Jameson shared his company's business insights with me because he knew their knowledge and expertise were the best in the world.

But he also understood that knowledge, learning and theory had little to do with success. It all depended on execution, execution and more execution.

By having us close to him and Mochi Media, he would leverage our power of execution and learn from it. In the end, Mochi would probably benefit more than Games2win rather than the other way around.

While we did not set up shop in the Mochi office, Jameson and I became friends and ran a series of trials and experiments together. A couple of years later, Mochi Media had a grand exit, and Inviziads scaled our audience thanks to our collaboration. We learned so much from our mutual sharing, which resulted in millions of dollars of value being created for both companies.

As I later discovered, Jameson was mimicking the attitude of the most successful entrepreneurs in Silicon Valley, many of whom even helped some of their fiercest competitors!

Bill Gates funded Apple and helped Steve Jobs. Jobs mentored Marc Benioff of salesforce.com, who said: 'Salesforce would not exist today without Steve Jobs.'

Bill Campbell, the CEO of Intuit, mentored Jobs, Eric Schmidt, Larry Page, Sergei Brin and Jeff Bezos, amongst others. In the book *Trillion Dollar Coach*,* based on Campbell's life, readers will be shocked to learn that Campbell rarely asked for monetary rewards. He just shared because that was his karma.

---

* Eric Schmidt, Jonathan Rosenberg, *Trillion Dollar Coach*, John Murray, 2019.

## LEARNINGS

- Sharing makes you capable because it is a natural counter to your vulnerabilities. By being secretive, you hide behind a veil of weakness.
- By being open and transparent, you become a magnet to attract top talent.
- Sharing creates culture. And culture creates an industry.

# 16

# The quicksand of gaming

As a child, I was fascinated with quicksand when I first read about it. My childhood experience with sand was with the regular variety. I would always wonder, 'How could sand ever be dangerous?' It was something we built sandcastles on the beach with and was the harmless nuisance that got into our shoes, clothes and everything else. One rinse with water or a vigorous shake would make it disappear.

Whenever my Nana and Nani took me to Mumbai's famous Juhu Beach, I would try and sink my feet into the wet sand, hoping to find quicksand (and get trapped!).

Nothing like that ever happened.

Only in my entrepreneurial journey did I not just understand but experience quicksand as well.

Gaming is like quicksand.

If you stand in it for too long, you will perish. If you don't realize quickly that you're trapped, you will be paralysed.

Even though you want to move and extract yourself, you will watch yourself slowly sinking to your death—just because you didn't move fast enough.

Over at Games2win, after quitting the MMORPG (*CT Racer*) business, we focused on online games. And as you read in the previous chapters, just when we began to taste success in online games, we were attacked by piracy, which almost robbed us of our precious business. Finally, great luck and exceptional engineering by MK allowed us to use the pirates and make them our partners via Inviziads.

The business seemed to be scripted for perfection. We reached a peak user count of ten million visitors a month. New global partners were reaching out for distribution deals. We even planned to localize and translate our top online games into the top languages of the world—Chinese, Spanish, Portuguese, Russian, German and French, to attract even more players.

All this would have made perfect sense and made us all rich, famous and comfortable, but that was not to be.

On 29 June 2007, a genius called Steve Jobs completed a lengthy presentation, and as he was winding it down, he said the immortal words, 'Oh, there is one more thing.'

That 'one more thing' was the iPhone.

The iPhone was the deadliest business quicksand ever invented. It would gobble up the Nokias, Blackberrys and innumerable device and technology companies that stood still and didn't act fast enough.

Online gaming was also a victim.

A year and a half after the iPhone launched, in October 2008, Google introduced the Android operating system for mobile phones, unleashing a revolution in the creation and proliferation of 'smartphones'. While Apple's iPhone approach was a 'walled garden' strategy (to do everything on their own, on their terms, in their own space), Google did the opposite. Their approach was to build a 'public garden' that allowed any hardware developer to licence the software and use it (almost) as they liked.

Slowly but surely, the new generation of mobile phones began to storm the market. As cheaper devices began to flood the world, smartphones created a revolution and disruption the business world had never seen before.

At Games2win, we initially didn't feel the ripples of this disruption. After almost three years, around 2010, it hit us badly.

Unfamiliar and troubling signs began to flash before us:

- Typically, the Games2win portal and those of our partners recorded the highest traffic on weekends. Kids and teens would start firing up their browsers from Friday evening onwards and would play their favourite online games till Sunday night.

  Now, for the first time, those weekend spikes stopped. The traffic chart was flat.

  Where had our weekend players disappeared?

  They were busy entertaining themselves somewhere else (no prizes for guessing where).

- More scarily, our Inviziads impressions of pirated ads (a count of our stolen games) began to slide down. This meant that the business of piracy of online games was no longer economical for the pirates. It indicated to us that players were tuning out from online games.

- New licensing and collaboration inquiries from international online giants that had gathered momentum suddenly began to dry up. Even when I followed up with the folks who had seemed so keen to partner with us earlier, they would not respond.

The business of online games was dying. It was in sunset mode. What made matters horrifying was that online games were the only business we were in!

In the winter holidays of 2010, I read an online article in a leading American financial newspaper that caused a mini panic attack.

It was titled 'What's under the Christmas tree this year?'

I discovered that this was an annual research article in the US, published a month before Christmas, which captured the most desired gifts children wanted to receive from their parents that Christmas.

That year, the most desired gift was a mobile phone.

It was no longer Lego sets, desktop computers, laptops or even gaming consoles.

This was our Games2win audience speaking out loud. They wanted mobile phones to play mobile games.

The writing on the wall was clear. If we were to survive and not get trapped in the quicksand of gaming, we would have to start making mobile games.

Changing my religion—from online games to mobile games.

The mobile games we had to now create were for a completely new range of phones. Their technologies, specifications, memory etc., were all different and brand new. These phones were not the Nokia phones I had made the *Sholay* games for.

This meant I had to start, learn, master and then try and succeed in an entirely new business line.

In the first week of January 2011, as I contemplated this new challenge, I noticed that online traffic to our site began sharply plummeting. It seemed that mobile phones had made their way into millions of households that Christmas.

The gut-wrenching feeling I had experienced when pirates began stealing our games hit me again. Everything seemed to be failing and falling apart. This time the situation was different. Very different. There was nowhere to look and find out what was wrong.

We knew what was wrong and what we needed to do. I just had no clue where to start.

Another Games2win board meeting was scheduled in the next few weeks. I chuckled at the coincidence. Whenever my business seemed to be on the brink of collapse, a board meeting would magically appear.

I grimaced when I thought of what I would write to my board to introduce the business update and agenda:

*Dearest investors and board members,*

*I have some exciting news.*

*Remember the only remaining business we had? The one that remained alive after we killed the MMORPG business? The online games business? The one that helped us invent Inviziads? Well, guess what? That business also died a painful death this Christmas. The iPhone and Android mobile phones have eaten our breakfast, lunch and dinner.*

*So, if you ask me, what am I planning to do to counter this disaster?*

*Let me honest and tell you that I have no clue.*

*Looking forward to meeting you and discussing our business.*

*Your hard-working, never-say-die, luckier-than-ever CEO,*

*Alok*

Of course, I didn't send that email, but its words remained ingrained in my head.

After thirty years of being fascinated by quicksand, I had not just found it but was helplessly stuck in it.

---

## LEARNINGS

- Business is like quicksand. When you become comfortable and static, you stand a high chance of being trapped by your inertia. So, the wise approach is to be uncomfortable when things become comfortable. As Andy Grove, the ex-CEO of Intel who transformed the company and led it to stardom, famously said—'Only the paranoid survive'.

- In my case, I should have been far more proactive about the iPhone and Android operating systems than I was. I should have grabbed those phones the moment they hit the market. I was lazy and didn't bother to look at a revolution that was brewing right in front of me. And the same sense of complacency was felt by the CEOs of Nokia, Blackberry (Research in Motion) etc. We all suffered terribly.

The wisdom I gained was to start using any disruptive technology from day one. I would urge you to do the same.

# 17

# Starting all over again

When you start something new, work non-stop at it, use the best of your abilities and talent, and give it your 100 per cent—you feel satisfied. Later, if your efforts yield the desired outcome, that feeling is incomparable. It's a high that has no equal. It's like being on top of the world.

But what if that high is suddenly taken away when you've barely even enjoyed it? If the situation turns so dramatically negative that it reverses all that you have achieved? How do you think you will feel?

In most cases, it can lead to acute frustration, anger and the sapping of your energies and determination. In the worst case, it can make you give up.

Now, imagine this happening multiple times, one success after another.

I felt just like that after having gone through the saga of MMORPG, online games, piracy, Inviziads and now smartphones.

In the first few weeks of 2011, there were many days when I felt like giving it all up and just disappearing. I felt like a zombie in the office, walking around without knowing what to do.

One day, while meditating, the third principle of my spiritual practice flashed clearly in my mind. 'The present moment is inevitable' was the sutra that kept appearing. It simply means that the present moment is unchangeable, so I had to accept it and move on.

The next day, my head was clearer, and I felt relaxed and motivated. I decided not to brood about the past or worry about the future. I would conquer the present moment.

The imminent death of online games weighed heavily on my heart and mind, but I pulled myself up and told myself, 'Alok, you have to move your business to mobile games now. There is no option.'

And that was the starting point of our mobile games business.

As I embarked on my new business plan, the first four months were hazy and confusing.

There were very few iPhones available to buy in India, and we had to rely on someone to get them for us from the US. They were expensive, and if we needed to make games for iPhones, I needed many of them to distribute within the company.

There was significant confusion about how these phones would get serviced in India. There were no resellers or authorized agents, and if the phone stopped working, there would be no way to repair it.

The situation with Android phones was even more perplexing. We had no clue which brands to buy and how to choose phones from among the various brands, sizes and specifications they came in. It was a circus, and we had no idea how to get a ticket!

But the most demanding challenge related to the change in the business plan was the product itself—the games we had made for so long and the new ones we were now expected to make.

Over the past few years, my team and I had become adept at making games for internet browsers launched on personal computers (PCs) and laptops. Our games' play screen was a large rectangle that occupied almost the entire screen. Players could play using their mouse and the keyboard's arrow buttons.

Now, as I began to 'experience' the new smartphones, I found that my creative ability to think of games for these small screens that were operated mainly by touching or tilting had been paralysed. For every mobile game I imagined, I could see only problems and obstacles in starting this new business.

One night, tired of feeling frustrated and angry, I had a tough one-on-one chat with myself. I told myself, 'Alok, enough is enough. Learn to adapt, survive and thrive versus complain and perish. Suffer that pain to make this transition. You will never be able to forgive yourself later for not trying.'

The following day, I assembled a small team and gave them clear instructions.

I chose ten of our moderately successful online games and asked the team to 'resize' them for iPhone and Android phones. The instruction was simple. Redo the art. Wherever a mouse or keyboard is used, replace it with a touch on the phone screen.

For instance, in an online game where the player needed to turn the car, they would use the left or right arrow key available on the PC's keyboard. For the mobile version, we needed to add a virtual steering wheel and then program it to be operated by touch. It was not an easy switch!

Five weeks later, I received the first batch of our smartphone mobile games.

They were terrible.

The art was pixelated, the screens were slow and static, and there was no fluidity in the movement of the game elements as I experienced in the online versions of the same games on the browser.

Even worse were the mechanics of the controls. The transition from click and point (mouse and keyboard) to touch (smartphone) was terrible.

In the car game, the steering wheel was so poorly programmed that the car veered violently to the left or right side of the road at even the slightest touch. Every turn resulted in an accident.

Each game was worse than the last. This was a nightmare on games street!

Slowly, I began to think through the process more carefully.

We divided the screen mechanics into two sides for the dress-up games and changed the orientation to vertical (portrait) for better gameplay. A simple touch would make the dresses appear on the model versus the drag-and-drop mechanics used for the mouse-controlled PC games.

For the car games, I hired an automobile engineer to understand how actual car steering wheels worked. In a week, he came back to me and said, 'Alok, you guys haven't added a steering wheel kickback in your mobile car game. That is why the game is misbehaving. In a real car, when a steering wheel is turned and released, it gently returns to its original position. That mechanism is missing in your mobile games.'

While he was right, it took us nineteen painful months (over a year and a half) to get the perfect steering wheel configuration for a car in a mobile game.

We also adjusted the sensitivity of the virtual steering wheel for different car types (sedans, SUVs etc.) and programmed different kickback settings for each steering type. I am sure we were the first in the world to pay so much attention to these small but critical attributes of gameplay for mobile games.

Six months after my revised plan on how we would make mobile games, we launched our first set of titles on the iPhone App Store and Google Android Play Store.

Now, there was a more significant problem to solve.

How would we get new users? How would players discover that Games2win had a brand new offering of mobile games for iPhones and Android devices?

While browsing games2win.com, it suddenly struck me that our traffic had started dwindling when our tween and teen players, who were earlier playing our games on their PCs and laptops, moved to mobile phones. This meant that the mobile game players were none other than our online players.

All we needed to do, then, was tell them that their favourite games, made by their favourite gaming company, were now on mobile!

We immediately added large banners and animated announcements on games2win.com recommending that players try out their favourite online games on their mobiles.

Further, in the ten online games we had chosen to migrate to mobile, we inserted 'also available on iTunes and Android' banners with embedded links that led them to the mobile versions. Now all consumers needed to do was click and download!

Unknown to me then, our cross-promotion platform of seamlessly migrating online web players to mobile phones was a rare and invaluable opportunity that was not available to most creators of mobile games.

Almost overnight, as if a switch had been turned on, we began registering a steadily increasing number of mobile game downloads without any marketing costs.

As players began playing these games, they sent us tons of feedback via emails, reviews and a contact form we had embedded in the games.

Most of them disliked the games. Since a majority of these players had discovered our mobile games via our web portal, they constantly compared the two versions and complained about how the online versions of the games they were used to playing were much better than the mobile games we had created. They sent laundry lists of problems, suggestions and ideas to improve the products.

While these messages were painful to read day in and day out, I eventually realized that we were in fact receiving invaluable feedback from consumers that would help make our products better. It was almost as if our product development function had been outsourced to our players, who were investing their time, energy and patience in making us better!

All said and done, Games2win had launched smartphone games in record time.

We had wriggled out of the quicksand of games and were now available on the platform that most gamers chose as their first choice. We had escaped death by inertia. Now, I knew that things could only get better.

It is essential to share that while Games2win successfully made this challenging move from web to mobile games, other online gaming giants, including our partner, Addicting Games, could not manage this shift. They remained stuck in their world of online games. A few quarters later, many of these world-class online gaming sites had lost all their consumers and had to shut down. Games2win, in retrospect, got very, very lucky!

## LEARNINGS

- I've realized that thinking about and planning how to start is much harder than actually starting!
  The mind makes all kinds of excuses not to start or to delay things. But things begin to happen when one can gather the courage to just do something, even if it is trivial and silly. If you plan to write a book or proposal, then on the

first day, just create a blank document and give it a name. That's it. If you plan to start going to the gym, then on day one, just drive to the gym and then go back home, or check the place out and be done. Just start. Everything else happens automatically after that. Lao Tzu's famous quote, 'a journey of a thousand miles begins with a single step', captures this vital lesson.

- Procrastination is one of the worst self-created diseases in the world. Luckily, its cure is entirely in your mind, and you can conquer it by willpower. Next time anyone asks you if you have any known illnesses, check if procrastination is one of them.

- A profound realization that struck me was that if new things are hard for one to do (like switching from online games to a mobile format), then they are equally hard for others! Challenging, impossible-to-tackle situations offer a reset opportunity for competitors to start from the beginning. Games2win was an insignificant presence in online gaming when we started, but in the mobile games space, we began our business early and quickly became leaders.

# 18

# Success at last!

After the first set of our smartphone games was uploaded to the Apple and Android stores, I devoted my time to making better mobile games.

I realized that the Apple and Android stores were a fantastic platform to do business:

- They had lists of the top-performing games by country, sorted by downloads and in-app purchases.
- The platform was free for publishers to post their games. There were no data storage charges for hosting games.
- The stores had a presence in many countries and were continually expanding their reach across almost all markets. This was the place to start if we were to play a global game.

Given that we were determined to win the global markets, I decided that the US iTunes store would be our only reference store. If we could win the most demanding and affluent consumers in the world, then conquering other countries would be easy.

As I diligently began playing the top games in the US, I quickly realized why our initial set of mobile games was not faring well.

First, we needed to think in terms of 'mobile first' rather than 'game first'. Second, we had to cleverly use some of the inherent mechanics of the new smartphones, such as tilt, shake, etc., to create games that would delight players and introduce them to a flavour of gameplay never experienced before.

I also realized that there was a fantastic opportunity to do 'freemium' games—games that were free to download, which offered small in-app opportunities for players to buy premium goods such as cars, decorations, dresses etc.

This opportunity had never been available in the online games space.

Further, the app stores enabled global distribution, billing, collections and payments, all for a small fee. This was a fantastic service that we could build our revenue streams on.

To produce quality products, I furiously began creating templates of game design documents that our product teams could use for thinking 'mobile first'.

While enthusiastic, I felt many team members weren't taking the opportunity too seriously. Apple and Android mobile phones were still fairly uncommon in India, and my colleagues thought this new business was a niche business. They were in blind denial of the massive change sweeping the world.

As an entrepreneur, it often happens that the more significant battles that need to be fought occur inside your company rather than in the outside world.

To get a steady stream of mobile games, I made it a rule that we had to publish at least two mobile games a month and also consistently improve their quality.

As we launched game after game, I prayed hard for something magical to happen that would help propel us back to gaming stardom. We needed a divine, destiny-altering intervention.

In the Bible, there is a famous saying: 'Ask, and it will be given to you; seek, and you will find; knock, and it will be opened to you.'

I did all of the above, and lo and behold, a miracle began to unfold for Games2win!

On a Monday morning in the first week of June, as I walked into the office, Dinesh, my colleague, came up swiftly to me and said, 'Alok, something unusual is happening. We released a game called *Parking Frenzy* on the iTunes store a few weeks ago, and it was completely flat regarding downloads. Now, there seems to be some movement on it.'

I ignored Dinesh's excitement. I knew *Parking Frenzy* well. Just before the game's release, I had had a massive showdown with the team members (including Dinu) over the poor art they had used in the game, which made the product look more retro than modern. Even though *Parking*

*Frenzy*'s gameplay was fun, it looked and felt like it was an eighties board game gone mobile.

The game was also one of our mediocre online performers and hence a test game I had chosen to launch on mobile. It featured a small red car with a top-down view (as cars appear from aeroplanes). The player had to drive the vehicle from various points and park in difficult parking spots. The game featured over 100 levels with tough parking challenges tucked away in cities, forests and mountains. Simulations of rain, thunder, fog and other weather phenomena added to the complexity of the gameplay. While the concept was good, the execution was tacky. Or at least, that was what I thought.

In the afternoon of the same day, Dinesh met me again and said, 'Alok, we need your attention now. The *Parking Frenzy* game is showing massive activity.'

This time, I paid attention to Dinesh's request. As I scanned the game's online analytics, I noticed a massive spike in downloads. Trained by habit, I searched for the game on the Internet and saw links to the old, online (web) version of the *Parking Frenzy* game and its stolen links. This was new for me. How was this old online game creating so many mobile downloads? I thought harder—if a game had begun gaining traction on a mobile app store, how could I discover what was happening?

Someone in the office suggested, 'Why not look at social media feeds? Maybe you'll find something.'

So I checked Twitter. When I searched for 'Parking Frenzy', I was stunned!

I saw hundreds of tweets about the *Parking Frenzy* game, many of which had pictures and link to the game. As

I reviewed each tweet, I realized that most were by teen and tween girls in the US going crazy about our mobile game and how it helped them learn to park in the real world!

There were pictures of real cars these girls had poorly parked, and then the same vehicle parked neatly after playing *Parking Frenzy*.

Some girls wrote, 'Our dads and boyfriends kept making fun of us when we tried to parallel park. Now, with *Parking Frenzy*, we've learned and shown them what we've got!'

Most of these tweeters were tagging their friends and urging them to download the game. This was an epic moment in viral marketing that I witnessed in real life. I was numb with disbelief. This was **our** game getting so much attention in the US of A! It seemed surreal.

What was most stunning was that we had neither promoted nor advertised the game. There was no PR nor any topical event that could have brought attention to the game. This activity was very unusual (do read the spiritual version of this story in my book *The Cave*).

Since the game was scaling fast, I decided to test it thoroughly and check if everything was working fine. While playing, I was dismayed to find that many advertising units were not working perfectly. If this game was going to blow up in popularity, it would generate lots of revenue for us, so I needed to fix the problem fast!

After getting my team to repair the malfunctioning ad units, I emailed Apple and told them that we urgently needed to update the game. (At that time, there was a unique email ID on which you could email Apple for emergencies. They would provide an app developer an expedited approval only once a year. I decided to use my yearly quota for this game.)

Apple responded favourably and fast-tracked our request. Our new *Parking Frenzy* game was updated and made live on the iTunes app store in less than two days, as opposed to the normal process, which took seven to ten days.

The next three days were a blur for me and everyone at Games2win. Every hour, we would refresh our browsers to check iTunes app rankings from countries around the world and would see *Parking Frenzy* showing a massive upward spike. The game continued climbing the ranks in the racing and games categories in most iTunes markets.

It soon became the number-one game in the UK and in several other leading countries in the world.

At around 1 a.m. (Indian Standard Time) on 12 June 2012, *Parking Frenzy* became the number one game and app in the US iTunes store.

Many other countries followed immediately after. Till then, no mobile game from India had ever become the number one game in the US iTunes store, let alone the number one app. (That record still stands to this date, as far as I am aware.)

*Parking Frenzy* amassed ten million downloads that week itself. In 2012, that was the equivalent of getting 100 million downloads today.

After the great rush and tremendous high of achieving a global success story, I sat down and again reviewed every tweet and social media message posted about the game.

An incredible pattern began to emerge:

- Car driving and parking games seemed to be as popular on mobile as they were on the web and online games format.
- This time, however, what was shocking was that over 80 per cent of the players were girls! We had never been able to capture a girls' gamer audience before, let alone millions of them in the US. Our mobile game had achieved the impossible!
- Players were sending detailed feedback, which was indirectly helping us plan subsequent game updates. It was clear that game apps were far superior to simple online games, which were played and forgotten.

For the first time, I said a heartfelt prayer to God and Guru for transitioning our business from online to mobile games. All my fears, resistance and feelings of hopelessness seemed so worthless now.

The Parking Frenzy success made me feel as if I was reborn. My investors were delighted and encouraged us to go all out on mobile app stores.

I quickly donned the hat of the chief product officer at Games2win. Mobile games, their user experience and gameplay were a new, unexplored field. It would be difficult to find professionals who would know what to do. As the co-founder and CEO, it was logical for me to take charge and set the direction we needed to rush into.

Over time, it became apparent that we had some killer advantages over most other mobile game developers worldwide.

Our online games and now a global hit like *Parking Frenzy* allowed us to cross-promote many of our new game titles and motivate our players to download and sample them for free. By doing so, we could drive organic downloads, which was one of the hardest and rarest feats on the app stores.

Apart from getting featured on the app stores (which required convincing the app store managers), there was no natural 'viral' download channel available. But Games2win had millions of players playing its online and mobile games. This was an invaluable asset that we could leverage to drive downloads to new titles.

Also, our Inviziads platform allowed me to compile a list of the top games that were commonly stolen across the most valuable markets in the world. A new benefit emerged all of a sudden for Inviziads. Now, it was a provider of global market and consumer insights. Something that the world's oldest and most significant research agencies would not have been able to achieve or deliver.

And it was entirely free for us!

I was astonished when I made the final list of the most popular games in the world. Car driving and parking, dress-up and story games were our most popular games across the top markets.

Getting dressed and parking cars were our path to glory and gold!

# LEARNINGS

- Success is a combination of many unknown and unpredictable factors. 'Why not try' is my secret mantra to achieve success.
- In the case of *Parking Frenzy*, a mediocre game enjoyed global success because it helped solve a problem (how to park cars) of a large community (teenagers) in a fun way. Everything that we thought was wrong about our game was ignored by these players. So also, in life, being perfect is not critical. Getting started beats perfection, hands down!
- From the depths of despair and darkness come the most significant inspirations. The piracy of our games led us to invent Inviziads, which significantly expanded our business. The slow death of online games allowed us to create mobile games, which earned us global fame.

These incidents made me remember one of my spiritual tenets, 'opposite values are complementary'.

When you have an obstacle, celebrate! Something better is in store for you

# 19

# Profits or revenue—what comes first?

Games2win was finally on the right track. After the success of the *Parking Frenzy* mobile game, my team and I created a solid road map for monthly releases of mobile games.

*Parking Frenzy* gave us a breakthrough and a clear direction. We saw a fantastic opportunity to 'gamify' driving and its complexities for US drivers.

In the next few quarters, we created games such as: *High School Driving Test*—a fun game whereby players drove and passed various challenges so they could ace the American Department of Motor Vehicles (DMV) test.

*Driving Academy*—which gamified over 150 real road signs in the US (including exotic ones such as pretzel curve ahead, animal crossing etc.).

These and other variations of games soared on both app stores and generated millions of downloads, all via organic channels.

Later came *Super School Driver* to mimic the real-life experience of schoolkids in the US going to school.

In the dress-up game genre, we added a *Super Wedding Stylist* game that simulated weddings in the US. That game, along with our flagship title *International Fashion Stylist* raked in millions of downloads, all via organic channels.

By the end of 2013, we had accumulated over fifty million organic mobile downloads. This was a unique achievement for an Indian company, given that 80 per cent of downloads were from outside India, specifically from the US and Europe. Games2win slowly and steadily began to get recognized as a brand in the mobile space, amongst consumers and within the trade (Apple and Google).

The year 2014 arrived with a significant change in the air.

The Indian start-up ecosystem began to gather massive attention. The elusive 300+ million Indian middle class was suddenly seen as an enormous opportunity. Start-up ideas to serve this mammoth user base that equalled the size of America began to look seriously attractive. (Circa 2023, as I write this book, still the 300 million number remains elusive.)

Famous, well-funded, blue-blooded venture capitalist firms such as Sequoia, SoftBank and Tiger set up local offices. They aggressively began reaching out to and connecting with young entrepreneurs who had a start-up or venture.

Following the 'what works in China will work in India' theory that my VC Clearstone also had, these New Age VCs began encouraging digital entrepreneurs to simply copy successful business models of Chinese internet companies and launch them in India. (Only a decade later people would realize what a failed and misconceived hypothesis this was.) These 'always in a hurry' VCs began to spray money at entrepreneurs who impressed them.

Amongst the varied cohorts of Indian entrepreneurs, the new VCs loved the IIT graduates the most. As a result, young kids who had never worked in a company or even started a venture before began receiving millions of US dollars in funding.

From hearing it as a pitch to signing final agreements, investing in an 'idea' became a game of 'speed investing', just like speed dating. The old protocols of conducting elaborate due diligence, product market analytics, speaking to market players etc., all took a backseat.

So began the Great Indian Internet Gold Rush.

A disturbing investment thesis of these new investors was the priority of chasing revenue over profits. VCs didn't want to hear about revenues and, even worse, how profits would be made. (EBITDA—earnings before interest, tax, depreciation and amortization—didn't even feature in many discussions).

They happily supported and encouraged ventures with half-baked ideas, a strong team and a business plan that involved growing turnover by incurring heavy losses via incentives, cashbacks and unprofitable offers. The classic example was the early food delivery apps that paid out more cashback incentives to their consumers than what these users had paid for their entire food order! Similarly, dozens of early e-commerce companies splurged money on trying to grow their topline (revenues) by offering goods at throw-away discounts.

As this drama unfolded in front of me, I too wanted to get access to this easy money. I carved out precious time, created a compelling story of the success of Games2win and met the top five VCs in the market with a solid pitch.

Each of these VCs met me respectfully, sincerely appreciated our success and traction and then asked me, 'Alok, how can you make this company grow 10 to 100X in revenues? What do you need to become a $100 million company?' (At that time, we were barely making a couple of million dollars in revenues, annually.)

I always fumbled over my answer. I explained that gaming was a consumer product business that must be crafted and cultivated slowly. It made no sense to spend Rs 100 in marketing a game to acquire a user and then recover only Rs 50 from them over time. That, in my view, was not a business plan. It was a plan to go bankrupt.

The VCs disagreed. They all had one message for me—'Alok, stop being old-school and conservative. This is the era of hypergrowth. If we're giving you a Rs 100 crore cheque to market your games, why shouldn't you give it your best shot? Even if the games make losses, we will have created a new market for these products. And when you create a market, everything falls into place.'

I guess I was old-fashioned and conservative.

I didn't buy this logic at all. What would happen after the Rs 100 crore ran out? What would I do then? Go back and raise more money? I asked three VCs this question, and they replied, 'Sure! We will give you Rs 200 crore more if you execute and show growth.' Their reply baffled me even more.

Another more significant challenge in my business pitch was my focus on serving the US and Western markets versus focusing on India.

These new VCs wanted to focus only on India and fund companies obsessed with the local markets. Their mantra was 'India, Indian internet consumers, Indian internet companies'. Revenues, profits etc., were not words in their dictionary.

I struggled for a few months, trying to grapple with these ideologies that were in such disharmony with my beliefs.

One day, I decided to sit quietly in meditation and pray for a signal on what I should be doing next at Games2win. As my mind gently slipped into silence and stillness, great clarity emerged. I realized:

- The most valuable companies (Fortune 500 companies, all the companies listed in the stock markets, etc.) made profits. The bigger their earnings, the more valuable they were.
- I had not come across any valuable company that had increased value by losing money and just growing revenues.
- I had seen VCs come and go. They were like the seasons. If a company's foundation was based on losing money, what would happen to it when the VCs vanished?

As my meditation ended, I took a few deep breaths, and as I opened my eyes, I decided that Games2win would place profits first. We would not bother about topline, hypergrowth or any other mumbo-jumbo financial metrics that the VCs were spinning out.

I concluded that I would not waste any more time meeting these VCs. This meant generating cash flow from our operations at Games2win to fuel our growth.

I discussed my direction with MK, and he was in agreement. We dove headlong into this challenge and focused on only one agenda—to build global games that made significant profits.

## LEARNINGS

- Entrepreneurs often feel dismayed (and jealous) when they read multiple funding stories about start-ups that have very little business or traction and yet manage to attract top-notch VCs that seem to go ga-ga over their bets.

  You need to introspect and ask yourself if the 'glory' of getting funded is worth spending the next decade of your life or more trying to execute a business that you instinctively knew was a non-starter.

  Fame lasts for a day—the pains of failure and doing what your heart doesn't accept last for a lifetime.

- Meet VCs and investors only if you have to. Else, creating presentations, writing stories and constantly meeting and travelling for pitches can distract you from your business, which will cause irreparable damage and harm. Measure how you spend your time and energy very carefully.

- Investors spray and pray! If they make a hundred investments, only a handful thrive, while the rest fail or stay inconsequential. This is their business model.

Simply said, they may not get it right. MMORPG should have been a success in India, as per my investor, but it turned out to be a big failure. In the same way, there will always be a disconnect between investor-sponsored theories and the market reality for all New Age start-ups when they start doing business in their specific geography.

You are the entrepreneur, and you should get funded for your vision, not someone else's.

# 20

# Getting arrested

My partner MK and I firmly believe in intellectual property and the legal, authorized use of any software or service we deploy in our business. Besides being honest entrepreneurs, the 'why' is simple. Since we build original intellectual property as games and make sure it remains protected and safe, it's logical that we respect other people's IP with the same enthusiasm and passion.

Interestingly, while this seemed crystal clear to us, I found the philosophy challenging to communicate and implement at Games2win initially.

As our business began to scale, we noticed that even after we onboarded new employees, they would try and work with the free versions of software, and then keep using different emails to redownload expired software using their official email. It didn't strike them to ask us for a few dollars to buy a perpetual license.

Further, almost all of them would exhibit strong resistance to paying for software (even when it was the company paying!). Instead, they preferred to struggle for hours using trial software and often tried their best to hack into a licensed product for complimentary use. They did not calculate the precious time (that cost the company in salary) they wasted just to save a small sum of money.

MK and I persisted. Over multiple company town-halls and in one-on-one sessions, MK and I explained to our colleagues that IP was the hallmark of any great company and that if we were to build IP, we had to start by respecting others' IP.

After what seemed like years, we changed the mindset of all our colleagues. MK implemented stringent software compliance IP checks on all the equipment we used so any potential violation would be detected quickly and eliminated.

The Games2win portfolio of mobile games began growing well, and I became far more confident about our business than ever before. There was pride in building an original IP from India that was being played worldwide. I would constantly talk about how 'software as a product' was the next level of software exports from the industry, migrating from body-shopping and IT services.

In retrospect, I believe I developed a certain sense of vanity with the product success we were beginning to enjoy at Games2win and the watertight IP controls (or so I thought) we had in our company.

Early one afternoon in October, an office manager hurried up to me and said, 'Sir, a policeman and some officers have come to the fifth-floor office, and they want to speak to you.'

The word 'police' surprised me, but I was not perturbed. I asked the office manager to send them to the second-floor conference room where I was sitting.

In a few minutes, a smart-looking Mumbai Police inspector in a khaki uniform sporting a one-star badge on his shoulder and a pistol in a holster entered the room along with three other men.

When I glanced at the three accompanying men, I knew something was off. They were shabbily dressed and refused to make eye contact with me. Thanks to my years of doing business across industries, I knew that these were troublemakers of a sinister kind. They by no means belonged to the police or any regular government body.

I welcomed them stiffly and asked the police officer what the problem was.

He said, 'We have reason to believe that your company is using illegal software, which is a criminal offence. We are here to search, inspect and find that software.'

I chuckled softly and said, 'Sir, there is no way we use pirated software. In fact, we are firm supporters of legal software and promote its use extensively. There has been a misunderstanding.'

The inspector was friendly and not looking for an argument. He said, 'No problem. You have two choices. You can either tell us what the illegal software is, or we can conduct a search and seizure operation, as the law allows.'

While I was confident of our standing, I also wanted to check if the action proposed by the police inspector was legal. I asked our CFO to check with our lawyers, and he immediately contacted them.

In the meantime, two of the men approached me and gestured that they wanted to have a word with me alone.

I was put off by their shifty behaviour and demanded to know who they were.

The rough-looking, pot-bellied one said, 'We represent international software companies, and here is our list of authorizations.'

He showed me a thick file containing dozens of letters from global software companies (some known, some unknown) authorizing this person's agency to represent them in detecting piracy in India.

Reluctantly, I agreed to move into an adjoining room and began a conversation.

One of the men cracked his neck first to the left and then to the right. Satisfied, he looked around and said, 'Sir, there is no video camera in this room, right?

I confirmed there were none.

He said, 'Sir, why don't you make an offer? I can make this go away. We don't need to do this and trouble you.'

By now, I was disgusted by this man and outraged at his demand. I refused to negotiate a bribe for something I had not done nor was even remotely guilty of doing.

I walked out of the room, met the inspector and coldly told him, 'Sir, please go ahead. I have nothing to hide. Search all you want.'

I also took pictures of the inspector and the three men. They warned me not to do so, but I felt it was justified to keep records of this intrusive and illogical action they were proposing. They shrugged and let me be.

The inspector wasted no time. He had called several local 'witnesses' to observe the search operation. The third goon seemed to be the technical person. Once the search began, this chap sat at each of our employees' workstations and typed various commands on the keyboards. I assumed he was running queries on the hard disks of our machines.

Overconfident that I had nothing to fear, I went back to the conference room and continued with my meeting. It was business as usual for me.

About forty minutes later, my CFO came to me. He said, 'Alok, I have spoken to multiple lawyers. They all confirmed that the inspector and his people have the legal right to do what they are doing. So, let's see what they find. I know there's nothing to worry about.'

An hour later, the inspector came to me and said, 'Please follow me to a workstation, sir. We have found a file extraction software tool that has been illegally installed and used by you. This is the software we knew you were wrongfully using and came here to find and seize.'

When I heard this, I remained calm. I was still not overly disturbed. I asked MK to check if this was correct. He was my partner and CTO, and I relied on him to keep our operations and business completely piracy-free. But when I saw his expression change, I realized we had a serious problem.

MK softly confirmed that a new intern had downloaded and installed this hacked software on his machine. It had somehow been missed by MK's IP inspection process.

The next few hours were a blurry nightmare.

Because I had not yielded to the inspector and gang of goons' demands to end the matter illegally, they proceeded to go full throttle and do everything they could to punish me.

More police arrived from the local police station, and many of our laptops and PCs were seized, along with hard drives. An elaborate inventory of assets was drawn up, documenting everything being confiscated.

I learned that the process for an FIR, a first information report, was being followed. This was the first-ever police matter in my life!

It was late evening. Most of our staff members had left the office. Some probably earlier, seeing so many policemen. Only the top management and the office boys had stayed back.

The inspector approached me and coldly said, 'I have to arrest a senior person of this company and send him to lock-up. Tomorrow, or the day after, the case will reach the court for the next steps. Please confirm who will come with us to the police station for documentation and arrest.'

The world collapsed around me. All the pride, the ego and the big talk of being an IP crusader and legal eagle were smashed to pieces. It struck me that instead of being defiant, I should have been at least courteous and soft-spoken to these men. Then it may not have ended this way.

I closed my eyes for a moment, thought hard and had a candid conversation with myself. I still remember the words I said to myself—'I am the CEO. I am the founder and owner. I am the person who took this arrogant and hard stance of being holier than thou. I am the person who defied a problem with attitude. And finally, this is my company. If I grab the attention for its achievements and high moments, I should also do the same for the darkest moments of the business.'

I did not doubt my decision. If anyone should go to jail, it should be me.

I told the inspector, 'Arrest me. I am the CEO.'

My team gasped. An office manager who has been my right-hand man for years approached me and said, 'Sir, I will happily go inside for you.'

I smiled and shook my head even though I was overwhelmed by his loyalty.

This was my mistake. I needed to pay for it.

And yes, as my company had used illegal software, we had committed a crime.

Half an hour later, I was escorted into a police jeep and taken to the local police station. My core team followed in their cars.

At the station, I was questioned like an ordinary criminal. I was asked to reveal scars and other physical identification marks. I removed my shirt in the process.

All this while, I was calm. A certain numbness had come over me. This is business, I told myself. You win some; you lose some.

In the meantime, my CFO was frantically trying to contact well-known criminal lawyers in Mumbai, but since it was past 9 p.m., many were unreachable.

After filing the FIR, I was sent to the local hospital for a medical check-up. Three policemen escorted me from the police station to the hospital and back.

In all these proceedings, the policeman and his staff were cordial and allowed me to keep my phone. I called Chhavi and told her what had happened. She could not believe I had been arrested for a single illegal copy of file-zipping software and was shell-shocked. Little did she know that I was partially responsible for this nightmare. After speaking to Chhavi, I managed to make a call to a person whom I knew was well-connected politically. He promised to help.

Half an hour later, while working on the paperwork, the police inspector received a call. It was my political friend who had managed to get the inspector's number. They spoke at length.

After the call ended, the inspector came to me and said, 'Sir, *aap kin bade logon ko involve karte ho* [which big people are you getting involved in this case]? I had told you to let me arrest someone else.'

I told him I was doing my best to make my case to him and the politician that even though illegal software worth Rs 3000 had been found on a company PC, it made no sense to arrest the CEO and send him to jail. More than my problem, I was trying to convey what the situation in the country was and how the justice system worked.

Something mellowed in the policeman.

He said, 'We are not sending you to the local jail. Please stay in this room. You can call for bedding from your house and home-cooked food. Also, we will send you to court tomorrow for your hearing.'

I slept on the floor of the police station on cosy bedding sent from home. The room had a noisy AC, which was operating at full speed, and an attached toilet. The policemen on duty let me keep my phone and didn't disturb me much.

The following day, I ate a home-cooked breakfast and also served some of the extra packets to a couple of folks who were in the lock-up. The police station had a mini jail to detain petty thieves and ruffians.

Around lunch, the inspector completed the extensive paperwork required in my case. I was told to be ready to go to court. In the meantime, my CFO arrived with a seasoned criminal lawyer to meet me first at the police station and then in the courthouse.

As we were leaving, I was surprised to see the inspector designate a young inexperienced policewoman to represent him in court. She was very nervous and didn't make eye contact with me even once. This was a strange development. Why would the senior inspector, who had spent hours preparing my case and proving his legal chokehold over me, abandon his moment of glory at the last moment? Why was he handing me over to someone who looked nervous and unprepared?

A while later, I reached the courthouse with two pot-bellied Mumbai policemen as my escorts. We were seated on long wooden benches along with the petty thieves, drug addicts and ruffians. They all stared at me as if I were an alien in their midst. I was!

Before sitting on the benches, all the arrested folks were asked to remove their shoes and leave them at the door of the courtroom (I later learned this was done to prevent us from throwing our footwear at the judge!). Two inspectors held my hands, their fingers entwined in mine, as we waited for my turn before the judge. The scene was totally out of Bollywood. All that remained was for me to plead, 'Meee lord'.

Mentally, I was soaking it all in. I had gone past the regret, the 'why me' loop of agony and the effort to prevent being seen or recorded. I had crossed the threshold of fear and shame. The fourth spiritual tenet flashed through my mind: do not be a football of other people's opinion. Yup. I was no football. I was in complete control of my experiences.

What kept me smiling and alert was the knowledge that we had done nothing wrong. An illegal download by an intern in a company of hundreds of employees did not warrant the CEO getting arrested and detained. This was common sense and did not need a lawyer or a judge to understand this.

I once again realized that this was business. This is what it took to build value from scratch. This was also the price of being arrogant. As an entrepreneur, it was just another day in paradise.

When it was my turn, I stood up and walked into the small wooden witness box and faced the judge. He was very senior and looked old. He asked if I had been treated well by the police. I replied in the affirmative.

He grunted in acknowledgement and began reading the case. As he flipped over the pages, the judge became visibly angry. He began scowling.

Midway through reading the FIR, he stopped and beckoned the young police officer who had accompanied me and was representing the police station responsible for my arrest.

The judge raised his voice and angrily told her that an arrest and detention for such a case was unwarranted and unnecessary. He was appalled at the way the police had abused the law and harassed me.

The young policewoman was nervous and kept mumbling in agreement. She informed the judge that she had been absent when the arrest was made. That irritated his lordship even more, and he demanded to know where the arresting officer was.

The lawyer representing the police fumbled in her reply and profusely apologized for the absence of the arresting officer. She could not provide any convincing reason for his unavailability in the courtroom that day.

The judge seemed disgusted at the police department and granted me bail.

I was free to leave.

After signing endless reams of paperwork, my CFO and lawyer escorted me out of the courtroom and to my car. Chhavi was sitting inside. Her face was pale, and she looked distraught. On seeing me, she instantly hugged me and started to cry.

My driver assumed I wanted to go home, but I directed him to take me to the office. It was about 3 p.m., a regular working day. I was the CEO of a business that needed me every waking hour. There was no time for melodrama. More importantly, I wanted to show up at the office and demonstrate to all my colleagues and staff that it was business as usual.

When I walked into the office, many employees looked at me, not knowing what to say. I smiled at them, sat at my desk and began working.

The message was clear. These things happen. There was no time to look back. There was work to be done.

Over the next five days, I conducted extensive research into my case and discovered several interesting things. A handful of old popular software product companies from the US whose products had commonly been used, such as file compression software, were now in financial jeopardy. Their original businesses had neither been able to scale nor survive the severe competition and as a result, they had closed their business operations. They had become skeletal outfits living off small trailing revenues from their legacy products.

White-collared criminal outfits (like the three thugs who had come to my office) had cleverly identified these software companies and liaised with them. Given the rampant software piracy in India, these shady agencies had promised to go after erring local companies and force them into paying for the legal use of pirated software. These thugs did not tell the US companies about the methods they would use to remedy the piracy cases.

These US companies could quickly identify the IP addresses of users who were using unlicensed versions of their software. The IP addresses in India were sent to these thugs.

Leveraging the official authorization from the US-based companies, these thugs partnered with local police stations to extort money from companies they knew could afford to pay them bribes to stay away from legal complications. A small fee would be paid back to the US businesses.

A case like mine was not envisaged. If it came to a stage where the bribe was not paid, then the police had to file an FIR to follow protocol!

A month later, I contacted the Indian head of the US software company whose software had been downloaded illegally by our intern. When I told him what had transpired, he was shocked. He apologized profusely and insisted that he had had no idea what these enforcement agents would do to arm-twist companies with such unauthorized downloads.

I did not believe a word of what he said. I was sure he too received kickbacks.

I informed my board about the incident and made sure they were aware of my arrest, the FIR and the legal case against Games2win. They were shocked and very supportive of me and asked me to do whatever it took to remedy the situation.

A month later, Games2win filed a case to quash the FIR in the Mumbai High Court. The bench granted a verdict in our favour less than five minutes into the hearing. We paid a fine of a few thousand rupees for the use of the software, and that closed the matter.

## LEARNINGS

- Pride, above all, destroys the greatest of men and women.
- When you have a problem, try and accept it first. Then solving it becomes easier.
- If you are an entrepreneur, know that weird stuff will happen to you and your business. That's the small price you must pay to earn immortal glory and freedom.

# 21

# You win some. You lose many.

As it should be, every story comes with some fantastic wins as well as big disappointments.

Here are some that stood out while building Games2win.

## 1. A chance breakthrough by Chhavi

As you may remember reading, while clearing out our kids' room I stumbled upon the family stash of toy cars, dolls and comic books, which inspired me to create car-driving and dress-up games at Games2win. These were immortal, evergreen toy themes that had passed the test of time. My inspiration was to transform these old-format toys into modern-day mobile games.

The third format—comics—remained unexplored, and I wanted to add that genre as our final content pillar at Games2win.

As I researched the market, I came across a few mobile games that featured multiple stories in a single game. When I think about these products, they were the 'Netflix' version of stories, presented as story titles in a single game.

One day in the office, I played the top story game in front of Chhavi and told her, 'Chhavi, you can start this format of games for us. You like to read and have strong English skills. Why not try?'

Chhavi looked surprised but then replied, 'Sure, Alok, why not.'

Even today, Chhavi reminds me of how I told her, 'Why not try.'

And try she did!

After several experiments, Chhavi created a story game called *Decisions*. Her storylines were similar to the erstwhile Mills & Boon novels and the Archie Comics series. Instead of presenting the content as plain text or comic strips, we artistically rendered our stories with rich art and compelling narratives.

What was unique about this game (and those of our competitors) was that the players could control the storyline and decide what came next.

As players read the story, they were regularly confronted with a choice—a decision (hence the name 'Decisions'). For instance, the main character in a story had the option to either 'date this girl' or to 'avoid her'. Based on the decision made by the player, the story would change and follow a unique path, leading to different outcomes.

We programmed many versions of the story paths and story endings, which was a nightmare for the programming, creative and art departments, but delivered immense delight to our players. They would replay the same story and make different decisions to see what the other outcomes were.

Chhavi worked to constantly improve her product and began adding two or three stories each month to the library, just like the most popular over-the-top(OTT) apps that add new titles weekly and monthly.

In 2021, our *Decisions* game became the third most downloaded interactive story game in the world (as per an App Annie report). To date, the game has amassed over thirty-six million downloads (3.6 crores) across both app stores and almost entirely via organic and viral channels.

'Why not try' remains my favourite line, and it can sometimes do wonders!

## 2. Who says ads are bad?

With downloads soaring at Games2win, an important part of my job was to improve revenues and generate profits for the company.

When I discussed the strategy for achieving this with my core team, the product managers were divided. They operated all our games as 'owners', and I needed their complete buy-in to my plan.

Some product managers felt that the real business in mobile gaming was generating in-app purchases (IAPs). They cited top games like *Clash Royal* and *Toon Blast*, which were raking in millions of dollars every month in pure IAPs.

The product managers also reminded me that since we had such a laser focus on the US and an existing audience, building on IAPs was the most logical. They wanted to build an IAP-first strategy to generate revenues and profits.

I had a different view.

Given that almost all mobile games are free to download and play, less than 2 per cent of players paid for anything in a game. (If you have played a mobile game, have you ever paid for things inside it?)

The 2 per cent conversion rate applied to the US— the most affluent market in the world. In almost all other markets, the percentage of paying users crashed to 0.2 per cent or worse.

My argument was simple: Why should we bother chasing a minute sliver of 0.2 per cent to 2 per cent of players who grudgingly paid for in-game purchases when we had the opportunity to focus on the remaining 98 per cent of all players?

The challenge was how we could make money from these 'freeloaders' (players who love to play but don't pay).

The route we adopted was to serve in-game ads.

From time immemorial, ads in games have been 'taboo'. It's like proposing to put up hoardings inside a temple to make some money. No one spoke about ads at mobile conferences. The gurus of gaming always focused on in-app purchases (IAPs) and dissed ads. The best case studies of successful games that routinely appeared in top blogs were only of games that minted money via in-app purchases.

Ads were the 'thing' that the lowly, downtrodden gaming companies did.

But I was not convinced.

The reality in the real world was quite the opposite.

For instance, the most powerful internet success stories worldwide—Google, Facebook and TikTok—all made money from ads. If ads were so bad, how and why did these companies continue to thrive? Historically, television, newspapers, magazines and radio channels had all scaled to be free to use and filled with sponsored ads to make money.

I convinced the project managers and doggedly began experimenting with different ad placements in our games. I had to find a sweet spot that generated money from ads without turning players away. I read all the studies and research reports about mobile games and ads that I could find.

As our downloads soared, our players complained about game glitches, level design problems etc. Very few ranted about having to watch ads. Why were players not complaining, I wondered, if ads were so bad?

And then, by pure luck, I came across a report from a top trade publication that shocked me!

It revealed that over 88 per cent of casual mobile game players loved in-game ads because they let them play the game for free! They also mentioned that great ads were entertaining, broke the boredom of playing continuous levels and even introduced players to new games.

I was ecstatic. This insight seemed so natural and obvious.

Now, all I had to do was figure out how to make the ads a necessity or a tool in the game versus a menace or something that players 'had to bear'.

As I contemplated this, a technological marvel in the mobile games ad business came about.

It was the 'rewarded ad'.

Essentially, the ad was a thirty- to sixty-second video that had to be watched entirely. Once completed, the ad 'rewarded' the player with a gift.

Sensing the potential of this innovation, we immediately integrated the innovation into all our top products.

All our games offer in-game items, such as fancy clothes, aspirational cars, etc., which can be purchased for coins/ diamonds called in-game currencies.

These currencies cost real money and are rarely purchased. Ninety-nine per cent of our players are content to play the game with whatever is 'free', even though they aspire to unlock the in-game items to improve their game experience.

Rewarded ads bridged this gap.

Now, we offered players a choice. They could buy coins or diamonds with actual cash or watch rewarded ads to earn them as rewards.

So, for example, in a dress-up game we have a gorgeous dress that costs 5000 coins to buy or the equivalent of $0.99. Now, we offered players the choice to watch five rewarded ads instead of paying coins to buy the dress.

After we went live, our players loved this new option and began devouring rewarded ads to get the in-game assets for free.

The popularity of these ads became so intense that we began to receive negative reviews and comments from players saying 'there were no ads available' in the game when their ads ran out.

I'm sure we were the only gaming company in the world whose players were complaining that there weren't enough ads in the games they were playing!

We had found an incredible way to make the games free, friendly and profitable. Our focus on three gaming genres, relentlessly improving our products and offering a blend of IAPs and ad-supported gameplay yielded fantastic results for the company.

Per our audited results, we had earned a cumulative profit of over Rs 65 crore at the end of March 2023 over five years (2018 onwards).

I had achieved my meta goal of making Games2win profitable.

## LEARNINGS

- When building a business, follow your instincts and apply your mind. What's working is more tangible than 'what may work'. In our case, I mimicked the age-old, time-tested advertising monetization model to make profits from our games versus trying to rely on in-app purchases. (Many Indian and global companies that went after in-app purchases bankrupted themselves.)
- More often than not, the veterans, gurus and priests of industries lose touch with reality. They become fossilized in their views and opinions. Listen to experts but do your own thing, because often, they are wrong.

## 3. Missing the social gaming revolution

Being intensely focused is probably one of the surest routes to achieving success. It comes with its disadvantages.

In my case, my world spun tightly around the three gaming genres, delivered as apps for Google Play and Apple App Store. The games were free and monetized with ads.

I lost out on significant opportunities as I shut myself off from the fast-developing gaming world.

Facebook became a fantastic platform for social games. Farmville reinvented the category, and Zynga (the company that made the game and several others) became an overnight global gaming success.

While social games launched in front of my eyes, I didn't bother about them much. As someone in his late forties, 'social' mechanics did not come intuitively to me. For instance, I couldn't imagine asking ten of my best friends (CXOs and business leaders in their fields) to look after the sheep on my farm or borrowing seeds from them to sow my virtual farm.

On the contrary, all my younger Facebook friends who kept pinging me to play Farmville with them became irritants for me. I shooed them away.

Social gaming was a pivotal change in modern-day gaming. It taught companies how to create deep social layers using simple game mechanics and extract tons of money from the most engaged players (called whales).

If I had launched a few social games, I would have learned the art and craft of social engagement very early on.

---

## LEARNING

- I should have played social games on Facebook even if it wasn't intuitive. I should have been the one asking for sheep and hens instead of shooing away my friends who did so.

  An entrepreneur should be like potter's clay. He or she should mould themselves to become what the business and market demand, rather than being rigid.

---

### 4. A shark throws me $10 million, but I miss the catch

Early in the great Indian Internet Gold Rush, I managed a meeting with a legendary venture capitalist who had single-handedly written cheques of over $1 billion to Indian internet entrepreneurs in rapid-fire funding rounds.

He had heard about me and wanted to discuss Games2win.

MK and I met him at the Four Seasons Hotel in Mumbai for breakfast.

The meeting started 8 a.m. sharp. The VC was impatient, arrogant and in a hurry. He did not bother to ask us if we wanted tea of coffee, leave alone breakfast. He was accompanied by his colleague, who later became the CEO of one of the most prominent e-commerce success stories in India.

Within twenty minutes, the VC asked me, 'Alok, which is the most famous Indian movie ever made?'

'*Sholay*,' I replied without thinking.

Games2win's business model had been crafted with significant inspiration from my meeting with the director and creator of *Sholay*.

Mr VC then asked me, 'Alok, which is the most successful mobile game launched so far?'

'*Angry Birds*,' I reflexively replied.

It was undoubtedly the biggest success story in mobile gaming then.

Then the VC dropped the ultimate bomb on us.

He said, 'Cool. Here is what I propose. I'm good to invest $10 million in Games2win within a month [he was legendary in speed investing]. All you have to do is guarantee that you will make an Indian game that will be bigger than *Angry Birds* and more famous than *Sholay*.'

I was stunned. In all our past meetings with VCs, the discussion on funding and the use of funds was always an entrepreneur-driven agenda. Financial investments were never predicated on a random creative 'probability'. It seemed this was more a personal, whimsical and impulsive investment decision than a well thought through, calculated and calibrated one.

His demand seemed unrealistic.

I replied, 'Sir, at Games2win, we aren't chasing the once-in-a-lifetime "hit". It's a flawed business model that can ruin the business.'

I lightly told him the story of Ramesh Sippy, George Lucas and Steven Spielberg and how none of these creators had known what they were making. Something clicked, and it happened. Even in the case of *Angry Birds*, the company

(Rovio) produced over forty games before they struck gold with *Angry Birds.*

The VC became irritated. I'm sure no entrepreneur had ever refused his offer. He said, 'Alok, sure, I know you will have to try. But you must make *the* ultimate game. That's why I want to invest in you.'

His expectation contradicted my belief system and the foundation upon which MK and I planned to build Games2win.

We both left the meeting promising to get back to the VC. We never did.

## LEARNINGS

- In hindsight, I was too 'holy' and zealous about my business philosophy. The VC became the most prominent internet investor in India, and many of his bets returned magnificent returns. As his investments scaled, his influence in the VC circles grew, and he attracted many new VCs to invest in India.

  Had I agreed to his demand, he would no doubt have introduced me to new VCs and strategic investors. It is possible that over time, he would have understood my business better and softened his expectations about creating that 'one global hit'.

- My problem is that I don't pay lip service. I never say or commit to something I don't believe in a hundred per cent. This personality trait costs me relationships and deals, and I am often perceived as rude and intolerable. But that's who I am.

### 5. A chance for a big exit

The Covid pandemic was terrible for the world but disproportionately rewarding for gaming companies. All over the globe, everyone was at home, playing games.

Starting from the end of March 2020, we began to witness download, revenue and business growth that we had never encountered before.

Each month, we earned profits of over Rs 2 crore!

The money just kept rolling in as players in the US and Europe began to spend more time than ever on digital media.

Later, as the governments of many Western countries began to dole out monthly support payments to families, household incomes rose. Some of that 'free cash' was diverted to playing and paying for games, Netflix subscriptions and digital entertainment.

In the early part of 2021, a reputed banker introduced me to a global gaming giant from Sweden. They had reviewed the Games2win business and were impressed by our achievements. The bankers suggested that I have a call with them.

I agreed, and during that first call itself, fell in love with the Swedish company. The team, their gentleness and deep understanding of our business were terrific. I wanted to align with them. I felt Games2win would have a fantastic future with them.

A few weeks of discussions led to the Swedish group making an offer of approximately Rs 350 crore (in cash) to buy Games2win. Additional money would be paid to the management team and ESOP holders of the company (employees) over a three-year earn-out period.

At the height of dizzy booms, the rational, logical mind tends to get disoriented.

Within our camp, we felt Rs 350 crore was not an excellent valuation for Games2win. Given the brand, the reach and our ability to generate millions of organic downloads, we deserved more. While the acquirer was paying us about 10.5 times EBITDA (a valuation basis), we thought that was a poor offer.

Our bankers also wanted to prove their worth and went about trying to source other offers for Games2win.

While a couple of term sheets came our way, a somewhat confusing deal came from a French gaming company that had been well-funded to acquire global companies and mimic what the Swedish company was doing.

I got on a call with the CEO of the French company and immediately disliked him. He was jumpy, irritating and even condescending at times. It was clear he looked down upon the type of games we made.

I gave my feedback to the bankers, who immediately relayed the same to the CEO. He apologized profusely and wanted to get on another call to clarify things. I reluctantly agreed, and this time the Frenchman was extra sweet and subtle. He positioned me as his 'global partner'. I found his duplicity irritating and fake.

In the meantime, the Swedish company wanted to press ahead with the acquisition. They tried to sign an exclusivity agreement with Games2win for a fixed period so they could conduct their due diligence and make us a final, binding offer.

Our bankers refused. The managing director of the Indian operations told me, 'Alok, one line in the contract here or there can derail the entire deal. I will not let you sign exclusivity with anyone. We will make them agree to a best man wins type of agreement.'

I agreed. At the back of my mind, I knew I would not partner with the French company, but who was I to educate a well-established, global banker on how to get the best deal for us? Even their fees were 'success based' (a percentage of the total value we received), so I knew they would strive for the best financial outcome for Games2win.

That plan derailed everything.

A week later, the French company withdrew its offer. They did not want to deal with a company in India without physically meeting us. And Covid would not allow it at that time.

In the meantime, summer holidays began in Europe, and the Swedish company's key management went on leave. When they returned in late August, their stock price in their local markets had begun to show volatility, so they decided to delay our acquisition deal.

That deal eventually never happened.

## LEARNINGS

- In retrospect, I think I should have taken the Swedish company's offer and concluded it without delay. As a start-up that had raised less than Rs 40 crore, an exit of over Rs 400 crore (including the three-year earn-out) would have been a great outcome. How often do you get an investment that provides a 10x return in a few years? It would have rewarded investors, employees and founders handsomely and found a fantastic home for Games2win.

- Trust your gut. Let it be the sole decision-maker when you are at a crossroads. As I have said before, listen to professionals and consultants, but make the final decision yourself.

## 22

# All is well . . . that never ends

The old saying goes, 'All is well that ends well.'

I have a different version of this adage: all is well that never ends.

Consider the current situation at Games2win:

As Covid began to wane, the world started to bounce back. As schools, offices, companies, industries and businesses returned to work, the old world order restored itself. 'Free time' at home was no longer a luxury. This hit the gaming and online entertainment business hard.

Also, the 'free money' disappeared. Western governments began stopping Covid social support payouts to families. Disposable income suddenly wasn't so disposable anymore.

The year 2022 was a year of heartburn and pain.

Today, everything in the business has begun to resemble the pre-Covid years. Everything but the costs of running the business! Our expenses have organically ramped up over the years, but with diminishing revenues, the fight to stay 'fabulously profitable' has become complicated but not impossible.

Is this another quicksand moment?

Maybe it is!

This time, however insane it may sound, I'm not nervous or petrified like I was before when things turned dark and gloomy. Now, I'm even more excited, driven and energized about Games2win and the future of our business.

What's the secret of this new inspiration?

The patterns of the past.

As I reflect, I remember three of the darkest moments of the company:

- the shock of our MMORPG business becoming a total loss.
- the trauma of witnessing our precious online games getting stolen.
- the deep dismay of watching our online players evaporate and migrate to mobile gaming.

These near-death situations made us innovate, improvise and become a more robust business than before.

The post-Covid period is another challenge that will provoke Games2win and our fabulous team to soar like a phoenix.

I already see trends and signals that will make us leap further ahead than we have ever done before:

- Our home market. India is now the largest market for mobile games in the world. And we have not even begun making games for India.

- Products as a service. I firmly believe that after software services and software exports, Indian gaming products will be the new heroes of the coming decades.

Why?

Because we have the skills and the talent, we speak English as our second language and are masters of technology. By leveraging Indian costs, owning our products (versus making them for others), and renting (versus selling) these products to global and Western consumers, we will enjoy unimaginable success. (Companies like Zoho have already achieved this in the business products space. Now, gaming companies from India will begin showing up!).

At Games2win, the recipe is simple. We have to do, lose, win, succeed, learn, improve and repeat the cycle again and again, just like we did in the past.

At the beginning of 2023, we crossed the magical milestone of 500 million (50 crore) organic mobile game downloads—a unique feat amongst start-up game companies.

## Peeking into the future

We will focus on building our portfolio of car parking and driving, dress-up up and narrative games. We want to go deeper within our specialized niche and be the world leaders in these categories of mobile games. I don't want to lose the vision of becoming the Mattel of the digital world until we become it!

Within each genre, there are hundreds of opportunities that remain unexplored.

Think dress-up games: we are planning new, extensive content sections of make-up, nail art, hairstyling, wedding planning, jewellery designing, and other concepts that are complimentary to this genre. Similar ideas are in the pipeline for our car games and story games.

If we keep doing what we have done so far, in a few years, I hope I have a sequel of this book to present to you when we hit one billion (100 crore) downloads and all the exciting stories that happened along the way! Who knows, we will be more valuable than the last offer that didn't work out.

Whatever the outcome, we will keep becoming better at our business!

# LEARNINGS

- A deep business question is 'what's your style? Going a mile-wide and inch-deep or a mile-deep and an inch-wide?

  In my view, as a business matures, and comes full circle, it's better to go a mile deep and stay an inch wide. Meaning—dive deep into your expertise (go a mile deep) and uncover value that is impossible for newcomers to find, vs trying newer ideas that may or may not be really valuable.

- Changing objectives is critical even though they may be been thought as being permanent. For example, when I started Games2win, I swore to ignore the Indian market and always focus on International opportunities based on my experience. But, given the rise and shine of New India, our demographic and economic renaissance, it's logical that I shed my 'from India for the world' motto to 'from India For India.'

  Having an open mind and never setting anything in stone is the big takeaway.

# Notes for the reader

Dear reader, by now you will have realized that my story has not been so much about fixed goals and outcomes (even though I may have wished for them) but about the journey of starting something, its highs, lows, nail-biting moments and incredible joys.

I've written this book to provide you with a glimpse of how I built a start-up and the precious lessons I learned along the way.

Let's take a moment to revise the key ones :

- Ponder over what you don't want to do
- Always place 'why' first
- Build small proof-of-concepts
- Be patient
- Never assume but always research
- Uncover key insights through simple observations of daily life
- Focus on building the best team

- Take calculated risks and fail quickly
- Never give up
- Always be humble and grounded
- Sharing means caring
- Remember that the journey is the destination

I hope this book inspires you to start up and create a business or service of your own. It doesn't matter if it is a success or a learning experience. What's important is taking the leap and getting started!

Remember, 'Why not try?'

My prayer is to read *your* book, which captures *your* entrepreneurial journey, experience and learnings, with the same goosebumps I had while writing this book for you!

Good luck and God bless.

* * *

# Acknowledgements

Games2win would never have been possible without My investors:

Sumant Mandal, Bill Elkus, Jim Armstrong, and Rahul Khanna of Clearstone. Rajan Mehra, Amit and Arihant Patni of Nirvana Venture Partners. Ash Lilani of SVB Venture Partners (now Saama).

My dear colleagues who built this company from scratch:

'MK' Mahesh Khambadkone, 'Dinu' Dinesh Gopalakrishnan, Tejas Shah, Satish Iyer, Jaideep Trivedi, Bhavesh Panchal, Manoj Yadav, Purtata Lew, Pooja Pandey, Raghavendra Upadhya, Ashish Sharma, Suprit Suvarna, Ronak Sheth, Haris Pathan, Raj Menon, Suresh Saroj, Salil Mahadik, Milind and Mihir Shah, Angelo Lobo, Vivek Manghnani, Kamalakannan J., Pranay Kumbhare, Viraj Sawant, Janaradhan Pawar, Shailesh Bhavsar among many others.

The incredible team at Google:

Vinay Charaniya, Sharan Tulsiani, Jaivir Nagi, Aditya Swamy, Nida Sawafi, Kanan Rai, Purnima Kochikar, Aman Grover, Mariusz Gasiewsji, Anand Nair, Guneet Singh.

The amazing folks at Apple:

Shveta Bhramha, Ankit Sharma, Anuj Desai, Ishan Vaish.

Mitesh Jain at Akamai, Sheetal Patel of Film Center and Rohith Bhat of 99games, my wonderful editor Radhika Marwah at Penguin Random House India, and dear friends Asha Chaudhry and Khusru Irani for the early reading of the book. Chhavi Kejriwal—my best friend, 'best half', mentor and guide.

Scan QR code to access the
Penguin Random House India website